Scriptural Meditations on Faith

Charles de Foucauld

Scriptural Meditations on Faith

New City Press

Published in the United States by New City Press
the Publishing House of the Focolare
206 Skillman Avenue, Brooklyn, New York 11211
©1988 New City Press, New York

Translated by Alexandra Russell
from the original French edition
En Vue De Dieu Seul
("En Vue De Dieu Seul" and "Foi")
©1973 Nouvelle Cite, Paris, France

Cover design by Edward Garza/Nick Cianfarani
ISBN 0-911782-62-1
Library of Congress Catalog Number: 88-61200
Printed in the United States of America

Nihil Obstat: Rev. John J. Brown, S.T.L.
Delegated Censor
Imprimatur: Francis J. Mugavero, D.D.,
Bishop of Brooklyn
Brooklyn, N.Y., August 10, 1988

Scripture quotations are from
The New American Bible, Saint Joseph's Edition
©1970 Confraternity of Christian Doctrine

TABLE OF CONTENTS

Foreword 7

Living For The Sake Of God Alone 11

Matthew 15
Mark 31
Luke 35
John 43

Faith 45

Matthew 47
Mark 77
Luke 87
John 113

FOREWORD

Charles de Foucauld was born on September 15, 1858 in Strasbourg, France. At the age of 6 he became an orphan; his mother, a devout Christian woman, died while giving birth. Charles was a very bright, but indifferent student, greatly influenced by the atheistic environment which surrounded him. His grandfather had enrolled him into a boarding school staffed by Jesuit Fathers. Letters he wrote, as long as forty pages, communicated to his grandfather the discontentment such a school caused him. At the age of twenty he inherited a considerable family fortune and decided to enter a military school and in October of 1879 he graduated ranking 86th in a class of 87 officers. The Inspector General made the following comment about him: "He is a remarkable person and has received a good education. But he has a big head, and he has no thought for anything except for entertainment."

He was commissioned a second lieutenant and was sent to Algiers. His lack of discipline continued to get the best of him and he was soon discharged. A short time later, notably more settled and mature, he was reinstated only to leave once again—this time for another motive. He was enchanted by the Arab world, particularly by its religiosity. Through the collaboration of a Jewish friend, he disguised himself as a rabbi and took the name Joseph Aleman. This allowed him to travel freely throughout Morocco and to make an intensive study of its history, geography and people. A few years later he returned to Paris. After a series of further events in his life he underwent a conversion. He knew he lacked faith, yet understood that he could still seek virtue. He came across writings that greatly influenced his lifestyle. The Abbot Huvelin became his spiritual father and in January of 1890 he became a novice at the Monastery of Notre Dame, and continued on to the Monastery of the Sacred Heart in Syria. In 1896 he was sent to Rome to study theology and in June of 1897 he received a confirmation of his vocation to "imitate

Our Lord in His life of Nazareth," where he went to reside the year after. This was to be his first stay at Nazareth, which lasted for three years.

On the day of Pentecost, in the same year, he began to write a series of meditations in which he uses quotations from the four Gospels to make a reflection on the fifteen following virtues: 1. to do everything for the sake of God alone; 2. faith; 3. hope; 4. charity; 5. humility; 6. courage; 7. love for truth; 8. prayer; 9. chastity; 10. obedience; 11. poverty; 12. abjection; 13. manual work; 14. penance; 15. seclusion. He did complete much of what he set out to write.

This book contains his meditations on the first two of these virtues: to do everything for the sake of God alone, and faith. They are not necessarily meant to be read all at once. They are meant to be prayers. His repetitive style of writing carves the way for his many rich insights, portraying a fuller understanding of the virtues and the Scriptural passages cited, and thus a greater awareness to practice them and to grow in their spiritual benefit.

These writings were not originally intended by Charles de Foucauld for publication. They were written exclusively as letters to a friend to whom he writes, "In Heaven you will see the depth of my soul, why not begin to do so right from this moment?"

Through the request of the Mother Superior of the Poor Clares, Brother Charles was ordained a priest. In September 1901, he left for Algiers. This time he adopted the garb of Saharan natives and made the oases of Beni-Abbes the location of his new monastery, where he lived alone, yet always in hope of receiving a companion priest to share his same lifestyle. "To have an exact idea of my life," he wrote to Monsignor Guerin, Apostolic Prefect of Ghardaia, "you have to realize that someone knocks on my door at least ten times every hour of the day—poor people, sick people, travelers who need a place for the night." Slaves fled to him for protection. His extraordinary life left a deep mark on the North African soil. In 1917 he was shot and killed. A letter written by the head of the Toureg desert tribe states, "From the moment I received word of the death of our friend...my eyes have been closed with grief.... His death has left me a broken man....

The marabout Charles has not just died for you, but for us all."

In 1933, René Voillaume started the first small group of men who would follow the lifestyle of Charles de Foucauld. They came to be called the Little Brothers of Jesus. In 1939, the Little Sisters of Jesus began their work.

These are just a few biographical notes. We printed them hoping they may contribute to the appreciation of his writings.

LIVING FOR THE SAKE
OF GOD ALONE

Pentecost 1897

Holy Spirit, I have often had the joy of asking you on this day[1]: *Per te sciamus da Patrem, noscamus atque Filium* (Grant us that through you we may know the Father and know also the Son).[2] And I am asking this of you once again on the blessed evening of a happy day. Since you have granted me the grace to begin to write these meditations today, a very sweet favor, one of your special divine gifts, please help me during the hours I spend on them. Be there and let me know the Son. May I know him better and better, love him more and more, imitate him better and better, serve him better and better, obey him better and better, and may he thus be glorified as much as possible by his humble little creation.

Sacred Heart of Jesus, I have devoted myself to you without reserve and I have given you my entire being, every moment of my life and all my works. These meditations are therefore yours, they are written for you, for your sake, in order to comfort you and to glorify you. May they therefore comfort you and glorify you as much as you wish.

Our Lady of Perpetual Help, Saint Joseph, Saint Magdalene, my guardian angel, Saint Peter, Saint Paul, Saint John, Saint Stephen, my protecting saints, please help me during these hours of meditation and prayer so that as they pass I may most please your beloved—our beloved—Jesus. Amen.

For each of the fifteen virtues cited, I will read the four Gospels in order, stopping every time I find a passage concerning the virtue I am covering. I will use each passage as the subject of a meditation. And the meditations will concern only one topic, the virtue in question.

---

[1] *Pentecost 1897, the beginning of these meditations.*
[2] *Excerpt from* Veni Creator Spiritus, *author unknown, c. 9th century.*

MATTHEW

1. "Hallowed be your name" (Mt 6:9).

This is how our Lord teaches us to pray. These words contain a petition for ourselves and a petition for our fellow creatures, for God must be glorified through us and through other people. But we must not want his glory, must not petition it, for our own sake or for the sake of others, but for the sake of God. That is why our Lord makes no mention of either us or others, but of God alone, God our sole purpose, for whose sake alone we must act, and who teaches us to say simply: "Hallowed be your name."

May we therefore have this burning desire for the glory of God for the sake of God, not that he needs it, since God is infinite bliss, perfection wanting of nothing, abundance to which nothing can add, but because it is his due, because it is righteousness, order and duty; and because consequently, it is necessarily God's will.

May we also feel the profound pain of sin, either our own or someone else's, the pain experienced by the saints, such as Saint Teresa. May we feel the pain not because of ourselves, nor because of our fellow creatures, but because of God: sin, while not hurting God, while not lessening his beatitude, is disobedience, an offense against him, unrighteousness, disorder, something contrary to his will.

And may we do everything possible through our prayers, our penitence, our examples and all our works, so that God may be glorified as much as possible, offended as little as possible. And not for the sake of ourselves or any other creature but for the sake of God (not that we must not desire our own good and sanctification or those of others, but we must want them secondarily, and for the sake of God). First and foremost of all, at every moment and wherever we may be, we must do everything, absolutely everything, for the sake of God's glory.

2. *"Your kingdom come..." (Mt 6:10).*

May your kingdom come throughout the world, may it come to every soul. May all people rush to serve you, may your grace reign in every soul as absolute master, may you alone act in every soul and may humanity live only by you and for you, wrapt in you.

Without a doubt, this would be humankind's greatest happiness. It is what we would most desire for our fellow creatures and ourselves, but it should be petitioned for the sake of neither our fellow creatures nor ourselves. It must be petitioned for the sake of God. As a secondary, incidental consideration, the kingdom of God must be desired in every soul for us and our brothers and sisters, whose duty and joy it is to do so, but it must be petitioned first and foremost for God, to whom the kingdom belongs, for the Creator must come before his creatures, we must think of him before we think of them, we must pay him his due before considering them.

"But seek first the kingdom of God and his righteousness and all these things will be given you besides" (Mt 6:33). *Our spiritual good and the spiritual good of our fellow creatures will be given us besides if we do purely what is most perfect for the sake of God,* and we will also be given temporal bread insofar as it is good for our souls.

3. *"Your will be done, on earth as in heaven" (Mt 6:10).*

We most desire both the greatest glory of God and the greatest good for people, for God, for our fellow creatures and for ourselves. But we must pray and hope for it for others and for ourselves only secondarily, and first and foremost for the sake of God, because it is infinitely right that we should seek God's good before humanity's good, the Lord's good before the slave's good. Since our ultimate purpose is the common good of the Creator and the creatures, we should pray for it for the sake of the Creator.

In everything we do, at every moment, we should seek, we should desire, we should pray *only for God's good,* since his good is the most worthy purpose our seeking, our desires and our prayers could have. And to be at one with God, we must, as he does, at all times and in all things, have the most worthy, the most noble, the most perfect purpose. (Actually, we and our fellow creatures suffer no loss because God's greater good, God's greatest glory, remains the greater good for humanity, the greater sanctification of humankind. Even if the greater glory of God were not the greater good for humankind — which is not possible — that would still be all the more reason to pray for the greater glory of God, to prefer God's will over the good of humankind. But the good of humanity and that of God are always united, and the greater glory of God and his will always mean the greater sanctification of humanity: "Seek first his kingdom and his righteousness and all these things shall be given you besides." *Let us only seek what is most perfect, the will of God, and God will give us our own sanctification and that of our fellow creatures besides.* This shows that while we should pray for ourselves and for others because that is our duty, since we are responsible for them and ourselves and because our Lord set the example for us, we must not spend all our time in lengthy prayers for them and ourselves but must do at all times and with all our soul what is *most perfect,* what is *God's will,* and firmly believe that our sanctification and that of others will be given us besides.)

4. "Give us today our daily bread" (Mt 6:11).

Give us, my God, the daily grace that is essential for our life, give us that angel's bread which is your flesh and your blood, give us that bread, your food, which is to carry out the will of our Father. And give also to all people and to us bread in the literal sense, in so far as it is useful for our souls.

We petition all of this from you, Lord, not for our own sake, not for the sake of other people, not for the sake of any other creature, but for the sake of *you alone,* for the sake of your glory, to glorify you. For your name will be all the more hallowed the more we, the more all people, receive grace, the Holy Eucharist, everything that leads to salvation, *for the sake of you alone,* for the sake of your glory, so that you may be as glorified as possible on earth. *For the sake of you alone, my God,* "give us today our daily bread."

5. *"And forgive us our debts, as we forgive our debtors" (Mt 6:12).*

My God, forgive all people their debts. I ask this of you not for their sake nor for my own sake, though I need such forgiveness more than anyone, but for your sake, Lord. I ask this of you for your sake because the forgiveness you grant them will glorify you: forgiving those ungrateful sinners will be a truly divine, a wonderfully glorious act, the beauty of which alone will glorify you. I ask this of you for your sake because you love humankind and the purification your forgiveness will afford it will do it infinite good. I ask this of you for your sake because you so command me by teaching me this prayer and in other ways too. I ask this of you for your sake to imitate you, my Beloved, because you prayed for it every day of your life in this world. It is therefore for your sake that I ask you: oh my God, forgive all people!

6. *"And do not subject us to the final test" (Mt 6:13).*

Could anything be more necessary than this for me and all other people? But I will not ask for it for my own sake; I will not ask for it for the sake of others. I will pray for it for your sake, my God. Do not subject us to the final test so that your name may be hallowed by the holiness of your creatures instead of being dishonored by their faithlessness. I ask this of you to comfort your heart. I ask this of you in obedience to your Word, since that is what you teach us here. I ask this of you to imitate you in your prayers, since you asked this of your Father for all of humankind. I ask this of you, my beloved, for your sake, because I want all my thoughts, all my words, all my actions to be for your sake. I want every moment of my life to be used for your sake, everything, and nothing either for my own sake or for the sake of my fellow creatures.

7. "But deliver us from the evil one" (Mt 6:13).

Deliver us from the evil one, that is, from everything that displeases God, from sin in this life and in the next.[3] We ask you to deliver us from it, Lord, not for our own sake, not for the sake of our brothers and sisters, but for your sake. True, we want to be delivered for ourselves and for all people, since being delivered from the evil one embodies all the graces of this life and the next. But we only want it for ourselves and others secondarily, incidentally, since our love, our hearts, the purpose of our actions are neither them nor us: the purpose of our thoughts, words and actions, is you, my God, our hearts and our love are in you; you are our good, you and your will are what we seek above everything else, at every moment of our life, and not ourselves, nor anyone else. You, my God, come first always and in everything. Whatever we do, no matter how good it might feel incidentally for ourselves or for others, is not for our own sake or for the sake of anyone else, but for the sake of you alone.

Deliver us from the evil one, Lord, so that your name may be glorified by every soul, so that you will not be offended in any way, so that Jesus' heart may be comforted. That is what we want above all. Amen. We ask this of you for the sake of your glory, so that your will may be done, for the sake of the comfort of Jesus' heart, and in order to obey you, in order to imitate you, in order to do good for your children for the love of you.

8. "But seek first the kingdom of God and his righteousness and all these things will be given you besides" (Mt 6:33).

Let us seek God, God alone, God's will, God's good, God's interest and benefit, God the most perfect being, let us seek what glorifies him most. Let us see only him, his will, and let

---

[3] *That is the consequence of sin.*

us walk straight. May we not consider any creature, neither ourselves nor others: What does God alone want? What is most perfect under the circumstances? What would Jesus have done? And let us do it, without considering anything else, without wondering whether it would be good for our souls or for the souls of our fellow creatures, and certainly not wondering whether it would be good for our bodies. If it is for the good of God, his will, if that is what Jesus would have done, it is enough. Let us seek properly, seek conscientiously, with all our heart, at every moment, what would be the greater glory of God, God's will, and let us do it. Let us not be concerned with our spiritual good, our material needs, or our fellow creatures' needs: everything we need for our souls, everything that is really good for us to have for our bodies, will be given us besides. Let us seek God alone, his good alone, his glory alone, let us seek to serve him alone, and our good and that of our fellow creatures will be given us besides by our gracious Lord.

It is right that we act this way: trees bear fruit for their keepers. Every moment of our lives, our entire beings, all our works, all our fruits belong to our Creator and our Redeemer. And his goodness would suffice, even if his Word were not there, to reassure us that such a good Lord would not let a servant, the servant's family and spiritual brothers—dedicated without reserve to serving him—lack the basics.

9. *"Stop judging, that you be judged yourselves" (Mt 7:1).*

When we judge our fellow creatures, it is never for God's sake, because he explicitly forbids it here and in several other passages. Not only is judging not for the sake of God, it is precisely forgetting God. If we remembered to act for the sake of God, if we kept God and his will in mind, if we focused on God, then we would not think about judging other people, we would not focus on them.

Ultimately, to do everything for the sake of God consists of having eyes for God only, to always focus on God. Then we naturally act only for him. When we love someone, we focus on him endlessly, we have eyes only for him, all our thoughts are about him, our entire being is turned toward him, all our thoughts, words and actions refer to him, to his good, to his desires: that is love.

To do everything for the sake of God, without doing anything for ourselves or for our fellow creatures, therefore consists simply in loving God. If we love him, we will do everything for his sake: our eyes will only see him, our thoughts will only be about him, and all our thoughts, all our actions, will be for his sake. We will not have a single consideration for ourselves or for our fellow creatures except to carry out God's will, for his sake. Oh my God, make us love you, and then we will necessarily do everything for the sake of you alone!

10. *"Follow me, and let the dead bury their dead" (Mt 8:22).*

Hardly any passage in the Gospel is more powerful than this one. There is hardly any other one telling us so forcefully only to be concerned with God, only to take care of God's business, to have only God in mind, not to concern ourselves with the rest, not to show any regard for ourselves or others, not even our father. Jesus called those who do not follow him alone, without turning back, without only looking at him, *the dead,* they are so far from life, they are so far from the truth, they are so far from the true path!

By citing the example of one of the most serious duties toward our fellow creatures, Jesus tells us: No, a son must not even bury his father any other way than for my sake. And if serving me, if my greater glory, my will, calls him elsewhere when he is about to fulfill this duty, he must leave his father and run to where I call him. Everything for me, everything for my sake: the tree must bear fruit for its keeper; creatures belong to the Creator. The duties they have toward other creatures, toward themselves, are only duties through the will of the Creator, and they must fulfill them only for their Creator, only when their Creator wants them to be fulfilled, only for his sake and in so far as he wills it. Anyone who does erything for the sake of God, who does not follow ...ising only on him, who considers other creatures, *is* ...

11. *"Whoever wishes to come after me must deny himself, take up his cross, and follow me" (Mt 16:24).*

Denying oneself is the first of the three things Christ asks of whomever wishes to follow him. Denying oneself means precisely not to have a single thought, a single consideration, a single word or a single action for oneself, for one's own sake, but to disregard oneself. We do not belong to ourselves, but as creatures we belong to our Creator. We are attached to our Redeemer, we belong to him entirely, body and soul. Everything we are belongs to him as well as all our works, our thoughts, our words and our actions — everything we have and everything we are.

It is therefore infinitely right that he tell us that our first duty is to deny ourselves, to do nothing for our own sake, to be concerned with ourselves in nothing, but to bear our Creator in mind in everything, our Redeemer, to whom we belong entirely, who owns all our thoughts, our words and our actions, in other words, all our fruits. My God, please help me never to seek myself in anything, never to consider myself in anything, never to think about myself, but to seek only, at every moment of my life, your greater glory, your will, serving you. May I deny myself entirely and do everything for the sake of you alone. Amen.

12. *"For whoever wishes to save his life will lose it.... What profit would there be for one to gain the whole world and forfeit his life?" (Mt 16:25-26).*

This passage tells us not to save ourselves, not to save the world: let us not seek to save either ourselves or others. Our goal, our purpose, is neither ourselves nor others, it is God alone. Let us then seek God alone. By saving our lives we lose our souls, by saving others, we gain nothing. "Whoever loses his life for my sake will find it" (Mt 16:25). In all our thoughts, our words and our actions, at every moment of our lives, let us thus have God alone in mind, let us seek God alone. Let us never, ever, not for one moment, have ourselves or our fellow creatures as our purpose.

13. "If your hand...causes you to sin, cut it off" (Mt 18:8).

If we devote ourselves to nothing but God alone, and if something he created becomes an obstacle in our search for God, let us cut it off. Let us bear in mind but God alone. If we realize that some fellow creature has begun to replace our love, our intentions and the motives of our acts to God, let us break ourselves off from it violently, let us mercilessly cut off such a cause of infidelity.

Let us immediately separate ourselves from anything that keeps us from going straight to God, from anything that tends to replace him in the motives of our actions, in the object of our thoughts, and from anything that diverts our concern from him, anything that tends to make us act for our own sake and not for the sake of God. We owe God all our thoughts, our words and our actions. We must keep him in mind in everything at every moment of our life and always do everything for the sake of him alone. That is our strict duty; it is strict righteousness: repaying to God what belongs to God, since he is our *Creator*, our *Redeemer* and the *Infinitely Perfect Being* that we must love with our entire being.

14. "And he said to him, 'You shall love the Lord, your God, with all your heart, with all your soul, and with all your mind' " (Mt 22:37).

The primary effect of this, the primary effect of love—perfect love—is to do everything for the sake of God alone. If we love him with all our heart, we want only his good, only his will, toward which we strive. And we strive toward his will, toward his good, every moment of our lives. If we love him with all our soul, we gear our feelings toward his, we look to him constantly in order to think, speak and act as he does, the way he likes most. If we love him with all our mind, our minds are constantly turned toward him to focus on him, to ask him what his will is, to try to do what he wishes, to best comfort him, to most glorify him.

To love him is to focus on him constantly and to do everything for his sake, for the sake of him alone. All our thoughts must be for him, for his sake; all our words must be uttered for his sake; and all our actions must be performed for his sake. At every moment of our lives we must aim at only one thing, we must seek only one goal: to think, to say and to do what most pleases our beloved Lord.

Oh, my God, may I love you! That is the only grace I ask of you, for myself and all the living. I ask this of you on this day, the day of your Sacred Heart, oh my Savior, since you willed these words to appear to me on this feastday. This is the greatest feastday for us because it is the source, in a way, of all the others. Where could your birth, your life, your Passion, the manifestation of your Resurrection and your glorious, happy ascension have come from if not from your heart? Your heart, which wanted to save us and comfort us, save us by your pain and your examples, comfort us through the knowledge of your glories: "What shall I make a return to the Lord for all the good he has done for me?" (Ps 116:12).

My God, on this blessed feastday, I pray for your holy love, for myself, for all those for whom you want me to say a special prayer, for all the living, today and in the future. May all love you with all their heart, with all their soul and with all their mind. I ask this of you with all my soul for them and for myself, on your behalf, on behalf of your heart, oh my Lord Jesus!

15. *"You shall love your neighbor as yourself"* (Mt 22:39).

You shall love your neighbor, not for your own sake, to satisfy your inclination, your feelings, your passion, not for the sake of your neighbor, but for the sake of God. For the sake of God, first of all, out of obedience, since he so commands; secondly to imitate him, since he sets such an example; third, out of love for him, by doing good to those he loves; fourth, for the practice of goodness. We must love and practice goodness for itself since it is one of the divine perfections, and the divine perfections are the very essence of God. We must therefore love the perfections in themselves and for themselves as being God. We must therefore love and practice all the virtues for themselves, and we must do so for the sake of God, because they are God: "*Deus caritas est*—God is love" (Jn 4:8), "*Deus est veritas et misericordia*—God is truth and mercy";[4] fifth, we must love our neighbor out of the desire for the glory of God, since our love for our neighbor and the good we do him, especially the good we do for his soul, glorifies God; and sixth, out of the desire to comfort the heart of Jesus, which all our good deeds comfort, particularly the good we do for souls.

16. "Master, you gave me five talents. See, I have made five more" (Mt 25:20).

This is indeed our image. We must not work on earth for ourselves: We are slaves and all our work belongs to our Master. He entrusts talents to us, but we must not use them either for ourselves or for others. They do not belong to us and we do not belong to ourselves. We cannot use them, or ourselves, or any of our time, we cannot do anything for the sake of others or for our own sake. We do not belong to ourselves, no more than do our skills or our possessions: everything belongs to God, everything we have and everything we are. We cannot divert any of it either to others or to ourselves. All of these things and all our time belong to our Master and must be used and spent only for his sake, according to his instructions, according to his will. That is pure righteousness. "Repay to God what belongs to God" (Mt 22:21).

---

[4] *The Scripture often combines mercy and truth as attributes of God, particularly in the Book of Psalms, for example, Ps 24:10, 30:12, 88:25, etc.*

17. "I was hungry and you gave me food" (Mt 25:35).

Our Lord thus gives us the true reason for charity, the most powerful. There are others, too. We must give to obey God's oft repeated command; we must obey to imitate him, he who gives so generously, to imitate Jesus who gave so much; we must give because the love of God forces us to carry the love we have for him over to people, his beloved children; we must give out of kindness, solely to practice and cultivate that virtue which must be loved for itself because it is one of God's attributes, one of the divine graces, one of God's perfections, and consequently God himself.

But the most stirring motive for giving, one that, while any of the others quite suffices, exhorts us above all, is that everything we do for our neighbor we do for Jesus himself. That is enough to change our entire life, guide all our actions, our words and our thoughts. Everything we do for our neighbor is done for Jesus. What an apostolic spirit that gives us! What a spirit of charity! And hence what a thrust to our prayers, our works, our lives! What a life of poverty, charity and self-denial! What a thirst for spiritual grace, relief for the soul and body! Now we can understand why we must be "men of courage" (cf. Dn 10:19).

What horizons open up! It places our entire life, both inner and outer, our prayers as well as our rules for living and relations with people, at the service of our neighbors, primarily at the service of their spiritual good, and secondarily their material good, strictly—absolutely strictly—purely, purely *for the sake of Jesus*. Because according to his Word we must believe with divine faith that *everything we do* to our neighbor, we do to Jesus. It therefore follows that if we want to spend our entire life doing the most good to Jesus, we must use our life to do the most good to our neighbor. Oh my Lord and my God, help me thoroughly understand this truth! Help me do the utmost good to you at every moment of my life by contributing every moment of my life toward doing the utmost good to my neighbor for your sake. And may I never commit any evil, any offense, any imperfection against you never committing—either in thought, speech or action—any offense, any imperfection against my neighbor. And may I do all that *for the sake of you and you alone*, because of your Word. "Whatever you did for one of these least brothers of mine, you did for me" (Mt 25:40).

My God, today is the last day of the month of the Sacred Heart, a day when I must think hard about your love for us and how to repay your love with love, to love you with the greatest love. Help me understand and practice how I can do good to you at every moment of my life. Help me make the resulting resolutions you want me to make. Give me your spirit, that kindly spirit you promised all those who ask you for it. Show me what I must do. Give me the wisdom of knowing your will and wanting it. Help me grow from the infinite teachings and the endless duties that your Word sets out: "Whatever you did for one of these least brothers of mine, you did it for me," so as to guide my entire life, produce all my thoughts, my words and my actions and to use every moment of my existence in a way that glorifies you the most, for the sake of you alone, and for your greater glory, my Lord Jesus. Amen.

Saint Paul, you whose memory is celebrated today, and who was driven by Christ's charity, and Saint Peter, you who told our Master three times that you loved him, great apostles who, by loving Jesus alone, had so loved others and been such great fishers of other people for the love of Christ and for his sake alone, I am entrusting myself to you both, since I chose you as my patron saints long ago so that God would help me order my life and use my existence in accordance with the light he gives us—among which the ones he provides in this passage are especially bright—show me how to govern my life and spend every moment in such a way as to do the most good to Jesus, to glorify him the most and to carry out his will perfectly. Great apostles, please grant me that today.

Blessed Virgin Mary, Mother of Perpetual Help, you whom we must always implore and to whom we never pray in vain, tomorrow evening we will begin to celebrate the feast of the Visitation which falls on the following day. This feast tells us how you silently brought Jesus Christ and his Gospel to those he had not yet enlightened. Teach me about your charity, about your charity for souls first and then for hearts and bodies on this day we celebrate your charity. In this mystery, you teach us to enlighten first, then to comfort and heal. May my life be governed and my existence used in such a way as to do Jesus the utmost good, to most glorify him, to do what he wants of me. I ask this of you, oh good mother, Mother of Perpetual help, you to whom I have given myself, entrusted myself, delivered myself once and for all so that you could have me always do what your Son most wants, I am asking of you what I am also asking of the Sacred Heart of our beloved Lord Jesus and for which I refer with great love and great trust and with all my heart to the saintly apostles Peter and Paul and to my good parents Saint Joseph and Saint Magdalene, as well as to my guardian angel and to Saint John the Baptist, Saint John and Saint Stephen. I ask of you that I may love our Lord Jesus with the greatest love at every moment of my life and in death, for his sake, in him, by him and for him. Amen.

18. "Not as I will, but as you will" (Mt 26:39).

Not my will, but yours; not my good, my interest, my benefit, but yours; not me, but you; nothing for my own sake, everything for your sake: your greater glory, your will; the rest, myself, let us not consider. Do not concern yourself with me, Lord, do not look at my pain, my sins, my aversions, carry out what glorifies you the most, whatever that may be. Do not listen to my laments, do not consider my suffering, but glorify yourself, my God, do what most glorifies you.

19. "But then how would the Scriptures be fulfilled which say that it must come to pass in this way" (Mt 26:54).

Jesus did not say, "How shall I enter into my glory?" or "How shall people be saved?" or "How shall people be taught?" or "How shall people receive the example?" He said: "How shall God's will be fulfilled?" In other words, "How would the Scriptures be fulfilled?"

During his cross, his Passion, Jesus had God in mind before

humankind or himself. That is what he said a few moments before, after the supper: "But the world must know that I love the Father and that I do just as the Father has commanded me" (Jn 14:31) and "If you keep my commandments, you will remain in my love, just as I have kept my Father's commandments and remain in his love" (Jn 15:10). Our Lord thus refers all his acts, including his Passion and his cross, to his obedience of the Father: this means he does everything for the sake of God, nothing for his own sake, for that of any creature. That was what he meant when he said: "My food is to do the will of the one who sent me and to finish his work" (Jn 4:34). And it could not have been any other way: our Lord could only have had the most perfect purpose in his acts. And since it is more perfect to act for the sake of God than to act for the sake of oneself or a creature, our Lord acted, in every situation, at every moment of his life, for the sake of God, for the sake of the Father, not for that of himself or any other creature.

20. "Go, therefore, and make disciples of all nations, baptizing them" (Mt 28:19).

We must not seek to save them for humanity's sake, but for the sake of God, who so commands us, out of obedience; and for the sake of God, who works toward that end, to imitate him; for the sake of God, the God who loves people like his children, and for whose children we must therefore do good; for the sake of God, God whom we must respect and love in people, his creatures and images.

We must love, practice and cultivate divine goodness for its own sake, because it is the very essence of God; for the sake of Jesus, who said: "Whatever you did for one of these least brothers of mine, you did for me" (Mt 25:40) and "Repay... to God what belongs to God" (Mt 22:21). Everything we have, our entire beings, every moment of our life comes from God and must be repaid to him. But by using everything for the spiritual and temporal service of our fellow creatures, for the sake of God, for the above-described motives, we quite perfectly repay to him what belongs to him, since we only work for his sake.

That last motive above all clearly shows us how perfect are deeds done for others for the sake of God, since our Lord sees them as not only done for his sake but done directly to him. Thus, when we pray for all people, it's as if we were praying for our Lord as many times as there are human beings on earth. Let us therefore act for many, for our fellow creatures, the way God wants us to, according to our calling, since that means acting for Jesus. But let us always act, in that way and in every way, for the sake of God alone, God to whom ultimately everything we are belongs.

MARK

21. "My heart is moved with pity for the crowd" (Mk 8:2).

Our Lord does not feel pity for them for the sake of humankind, but for the sake of God, because *it is good*, because it is *divine* to be merciful, to be compassionate, to be charitable, to be good. That is part of goodness, and goodness is a divine attribute, it is God himself. Our Lord feels pity for people for other reasons too, but always, always for the sake of God. All persons are creatures of God of great beauty that came from his hands and were made in his image. This is why we should love humanity and feel pity for all people for the sake of God. All persons are loved by the Father out of divine goodness and because they are his creatures made in his likeness. That is also a motive for Jesus to love people for the sake of God.

In his Holy Books, God ordered people to show charity, mercy and compassion for each other. That is one reason why Jesus' human soul is charitable, merciful, loving and compassionate toward people for the sake of God. God is good to both the good and the bad. At every moment he showers all people with blessings. Jesus, who said to us: "So be perfect, just as your heavenly Father is perfect" (Mt 5:48), is the first to imitate the heavenly Father he cites as an example. Such imitation is another reason for him to be loving and compassionate and to feel pity for us for the sake of God. But Jesus never acts for the sake of humankind, always for the sake of God, since at all times his purpose is the most noble, the highest, the most perfect, and that purpose can only be God.

22. "Whoever wishes to come after me must deny himself, take up his cross, and follow me" (Mk 8:34).

The first thing Jesus asks of those who wish to be his disciples is to deny themselves and consequently to do nothing for their own sake. It is understood that they must deny themselves so that they think only about God. They must give up themselves absolutely, give up their interests, their good, their benefit, in order to devote themselves entirely to God, to his interest, to his good, to his benefit. They must cease focusing on themselves, and do nothing for their own sake, so that they focus on God alone and do everything for his sake alone. That is the first condition to becoming a disciple of Jesus.

23. "For whoever wishes to save his life will lose it, but whoever loses his life for my sake and that of the Gospel's will save it" (Mk 8:35).

He who seeks to save his own life will lose it; he who seeks God will save it. He who seeks his own good, his own interest or his own spiritual or material benefit loses his life, while he who seeks the good, the interest and the benefit of God will save his life. This is because he who seeks his own spiritual or material good instead of God's commits an offense since he owes himself to God: the tree must bear fruit for its keeper and has no right to divert its fruit for its own use. In addition, he commits a folly by loving himself more than he loves God, because loving such an inferior being more than higher perfection is madness. He who acts for his own sake loses his life, and he who acts for the sake of God saves his life.

To do everything for the sake of God is right. We received everything from God, our Creator and our Redeemer, and we must render everything to him. That is wisdom, for wisdom consists of infinitely loving only beauty and sovereign perfection and consequently to refer everything to such perfection, to live and breath only for it. In truth, we can and *must* seek our own spiritual benefit, and even our temporal benefit to a certain extent, but *not for our own sake, but for the sake of God alone*, because God so commanded us, because God loves us, because it is important for his greater glory.

24. "If your hand causes you to sin, cut it off" (Mk 9:43).

If your hand prevents you from acting for the sake of God only, cut it off. If your hand prompts you to act for its own sake, for your own sake or for the sake of some other creature, if it is too dear to you and causes you to focus on it and divert your attention from God; if it is too dear to you and leads you to cease loving God, but to love your hand, to want it, to seek it for its own sake, then cut it off. In other words, if your hand seems to be taking over part—no matter how small a part—of your heart, your soul, your mind, your strength, all of which you owe entirely to God, if it is making you love it for its own sake, making you act—no matter how little—for its own sake, then in that case your hand is causing you to be unfaithful to God, and you must cut it off, cut it off immediately. For God is your Creator, your Redeemer, to whom you owe everything you are and everything you have. Repay to God what is God's, and you owe God, the supreme beauty, all your love, all your thoughts, all your aspirations and all your attention.

25. "Repay...to God what is God's" (Mk 12:17).

God made us whole, body and soul, so we owe him as our Creator everything we are, both body and soul, all our thoughts, our words and our actions. God keeps us constantly through his Providence: by his Providence alone can our bodies and souls subsist and act. We therefore owe him as our Keeper all the movements of our bodies and of our souls, all our thoughts, our words and our actions.

God redeemed us. If not for our Lord Jesus we would be eternally dead for he gave our souls new life. We therefore owe him all the movements of our souls, which have no life but through him as our Redeemer, all our thoughts, our words and our actions. God is infinite beauty, supreme perfection, the infinitely loveable being. We therefore owe him, out of righteousness and wisdom, to love him with all our strength, all our souls, all our heart and all our mind, and consequently, according to the rules of love, to think, speak and act only for his sake. We must therefore refer all our thoughts, our words and our actions to God as our Beloved.

Repaying to God what is God's thus means living only for him, having thoughts, words and actions for his sake alone, focusing on him alone, doing everything, absolutely everything, for his sake alone.

26. "You shall love the Lord your God with all your heart, with all your soul, with all your mind, and with all your strength" (Mk 12:30).

This command necessarily requires that we do everything for the sake of God, that all our thoughts, our words and our actions be carried out for the sake of God. When we love someone, we focus only on our beloved, our minds are only concerned with that being; our sovereign desire above everything else is for the good of our beloved, and that desire fills our entire heart, occupies it entirely. All the forces of our soul and all the strength of our body are geared toward a single goal: providing to the greatest extent possible for the good of our beloved. To focus only on our beloved, to do everything for the sake of our beloved, is an inviolable law of love. Let us thus do everything for the sake of God alone, absolutely everything—thoughts, words, actions—to love him perfectly.

LUKE

27. "Behold, I am the handmaid of the Lord" (Lk 1:38).

This is what we must tell ourselves every moment of our life, and every moment of our life we must prove ourselves the Lord's handmaid by working for him, by acting for his sake.

28. "Did you not know that I must be in my Father's house?" (Lk 2:49).

I must not be primarily concerned with my earthly mother and father, and even less concerned with another creature or myself, but with my Father in heaven. I must act not for my earthly parents' sake, for any human's sake, or for my own sake, but for the sake of the heavenly Father. I must do everything for his sake alone, without the slightest consideration for anything that hinders his greater glory. His greater glory is what keeps me here in Jerusalem, despite the obedience and love that are calling me to my parents' side. What do parents matter when God speaks? I focus on God alone; I do everything for his sake alone; I am staying in Jerusalem. I am staying for his greater glory without notifying my parents, despite their concern and their tears; everything for the sake of God alone—his greater glory above all. That is all I am concerned with, the rest has disappeared, and I am staying without sending word.

For his greater glory I have let my parents search for me for three days without informing them of my presence in the temple, which would be so easy. I am only concerned with the greater glory of God above all else. Next to that, everything else is nought. Next to the Creator, what is a creature? Doing everything for the sake of God alone, I am staying and am not sending word. And the same could be said for every moment in the life of Jesus. He told everyone: What are creatures next to the Creator? He told everyone: Do everything for the sake of God alone. He did everything for everyone for the sake of God alone.

29. *"He must deny himself, take up his cross daily and follow me" (Lk 9:23).*

The first condition to becoming a disciple of Jesus is to deny oneself, to set aside one's own interests, one's own benefit, one's own good, and to think only about the interests, benefit and good of God. Not that it is a sin to seek one's own interest, one's own good, one's own salvation or one's spiritual and even material benefit—not at all—but the point here is not to determine what is sin and what is not, but to seek what is most perfect, what we must do to love God with the greatest love. We are not concerned with what is allowed or not, we are seeking what is best, what is holiest, what is most perfect.

It is good to seek one's salvation for one's own sake; it is good to seek the salvation of our neighbors for our neighbors' sake; it is good to seek—within reasonable limits—one's material benefit and the material benefit of one's neighbor for one's own sake and for the sake of others, but that is all far from perfect. It is far more perfect to cry with David: "Praise, you servants of the Lord, praise the name of the Lord" (Ps 113:1). Do not be concerned with us Lord, not with us, but with your glory. May we forget about ourselves and only think about you. May we forget our interests and seek only yours. May we forget our benefits, our good, we creatures, and seek only your benefit, your good, and think only about you.

In truth, we will still seek to save ourselves more than ever, since our motive will be higher, more powerful. But it will be for your sake and no longer for our own sake. We will still seek the salvation of our fellow creatures, and more than ever, since our motive will be higher, more worthy, more stimulating, but it will be for your sake and no longer for the sake of our fellow creatures. We will still seek the material welfare of others and even of ourselves, to the extent you so wish us to, but it will no longer be for others or for ourselves, but for your sake, to please you, to do your will.

We will do everything for your sake, my God, we will forget ourselves, because it is more perfect to act in everything for the most worthy purpose, and there is no purpose more worthy than you, my God. We will do everything for your sake, because the First Commandment is to love you with all our being. And when someone loves that way he forgets all the rest and does everything, absolutely everything, for the sake of his beloved. We will do everything for your sake, because even though you allow us to act for our own sake and for the sake of others as long as we remain within the limits of your commandments and are subject to your obedience, it is nevertheless more righteous and appreciative to do everything not only subject to your will, but purely for your sake alone, since everything, absolutely everything, comes to us from you alone, from our Creator and our beloved Redeemer.

30. "Whoever wishes to save his life will lose it, but whoever loses his life for my sake will save it" (Lk 9:24).

Let us lose our soul for Jesus by forgetting our life, by no longer seeking either the interests or good of our life, by no longer performing any of our acts for the sake of our life, by no longer having a single thought, a single word or a single act for the sake our own life, but let all our thoughts, our words and our acts be for the sake of Jesus alone. Let us lose our soul, let us forget it, let us disregard it to that point, to the point of no longer using a single second, a single moment of our entire lives for the sake of our soul, but may all our moments, without the exception of a single second, be used for the sake of God alone. We will thus lose our lives for him, will thus love him with the greatest love, we will thus fully repay to him what belongs to him, that is, everything we are and every moment of our lives.

31. "Father, hallowed be your name" (Lk 11:2-4).

Hallowed be your name, my God, I pray for your sake.

Seeking your glory, obtaining your glory, and doing so for your sake is my purpose, my necessary purpose, like that of all your works, for you yourself can only have the most perfect purpose in all your works. That purpose is your glory for your sake alone. It is the most perfect purpose because it is the most worthy, and because it is right. Your kingdom come, in all souls and in mine. This I ask of you for your sake, for your glory, for the comfort of your heart, which are the main goals I seek. Give us this day our daily bread, your grace, the Holy Eucharist, the grace of doing your will. As for the rest, I also expect it from you alone, but I am not asking for it, because you promised me that it would be given me besides if I faithfully seek your kingdom and the fulfillment of your will.

Forgive us, forgive me, my sins, I ask of you for your sake, for your glory, for the manifestation of your mercy, for the purity of your children, so that once purified they might better serve you, for your comfort, because your heart loves your children, for the fulfillment of your will in them, since your will is for the sinner not to perish but to convert and live.

And do not subject us to the final test, I ask of you for your sake, since you command me to pray for all people, since you set the example for me during your life on earth, since you love all people and I must therefore love them and do good to them for your sake, since all people are your creatures and your images, two reasons for me to love them for your sake, because you are goodness itself.

I must therefore love, cultivate and practice goodness for itself because it is divine, and consequently practice it with all people, since whatever I do for one of these least brothers of yours, I do it for Jesus (cf. Mt 25:40), since it is my purpose — my secondary, partial purpose — to work toward the salvation of all people for your sake. My primary purpose is to glorify you. In order to glorify you I must first sanctify myself; secondly, I must sanctify my neighbor as well as I can. Praying for all people is therefore part of my secondary purpose, and I must do this for your greater glory, which is my main purpose.

32. "Whoever is not with me is against me, and whoever does not gather with me scatters" (Lk 11:23).

My God, please explain this Word to me and help me understand how it can apply to some extent to the duty to do everything for your sake. Doing everything for your sake is not an absolute duty, and not doing everything for your sake is not a sin as long as it is not for a bad purpose, a forbidden one, but then it would be imperfect. I am only concerned with what is most perfect here, since that is what I want always, my God, to do everything for your sake, everything, absolutely everything, out of righteousness and out of love.

The person who is not with you is against you; the person who is not God's handmaid, who does not seek good, who does not act according to one's conscience, is the devil's handmaid. There are only two banners on this earth, as in the other world there are only two states, that of the chosen and that of the damned. One can be with you without doing everything for your sake, since you so allow it to be, but the more one does for your sake, the more one is a good soldier, a faithful friend, the more one is with you; the less one acts for your sake, while not sinning, the more one is a tepid soldier, an indifferent friend, the less one will be *near* you, while still *with* you.

The person who does not gather with you, scatters. The person who does not gather worthiness with you by serving you loses his time and will find oneself empty-handed when the Master asks an account for the talents one has been entrusted. The more one acts for your sake, the more one gathers with you, the more abundant a harvest one will have to present to the Master. The less one acts for your sake, the less one gathers, the less worthiness one harvests, the less one has to show at the end of the day. Something can nevertheless be gathered, since you allow it to be that way, but it will be a meager harvest, so different from the one that could have been reaped by acting for your sake, that in seeing the difference one could not help but realize that whoever acts otherwise than for your sake, while not sinning, is losing one's time, is scattering instead of gathering. With much effort and toil, a person can gather a thin handful of wheat, whereas by doing everything for your sake this same person would have happily harvested a nice bundle. Acting for oneself or for other creatures is a waste of time. Let us do everything for your sake alone, my God. That is what is most loving, most righteous, most perfect. Bless us with doing everything for your sake. Amen.

33. *"Instead, seek his kingdom, and these other things will be given you besides" (Lk 12:31).*

Let us first seek the glory of God, and all the rest will be given us besides. Let us do everything for the sake of God's glory, and let us not worry about anything else, not even about our own salvation or that of our neighbor. If we do everything for the sake of God's glory, if we seek his greater glory in everything, God will give us both our salvation and that of our neighbor and of a multitude of souls, and all the other things we need besides. Could such a good Master let his servant, who is entirely devoted to his service and works night and day for him with absolute dedication, lack the basics?

34. *"I have come to set the earth on fire, and how I wish it were already blazing!" (Lk 12:49).*

It is the fire of love, oh my God, that you came to set on earth, that is what you wish to be blazing. It will burn in us if, and only if, we do everything, if we perform every single act, for the sake of God, every single act to most glorify him, if we seek at every moment of our lives to please him as best possible. That is a law of love: love focuses constantly on its object, its thoughts do not stray anywhere else, love does everything for the sake of its object, and in everything it seeks the good of the beloved entity.

Oh my God, you who in your infinite goodness not only did me so much good during your mortal life, having carried the cross and been crucified for me, having prayed, worked and suffered so much for me in Nazareth, tonight you are also granting me the sweet grace of being at your feet, of talking with you, here at our feet in such a sweet *tete-a-tete.* You who are here with me, my God, against whom I am leaning, to whom I am speaking, oh my God, set me on fire, the fire of your love that breathes only for you, that thinks only of you, that thinks only for your sake, that speaks only for your sake, that acts only for your sake, that at every moment sees you and seeks to do what will most glorify you, what is most perfect, your will, what you most want, what comforts you most, and does so for the sake of you alone, for you and not for itself, for your glory, your comfort and not for its own good, for you alone, my God, through this selfless love that in everything seeks only the good of its beloved object.

35. "If anyone comes to me without hating his father and mother, wife and children, brothers and sisters, and even his own life, he cannot be my disciple" (Lk 14:26).

What does that mean? My God, explain it to me, please, and show me how it relates to the duty of love that consists of doing everything for your sake.

It means that you must not love your father, mother or any other creature more than me. That is, you must never do anything that I would not like because of them, never place their good above my will. That is what is necessary. But the perfection of this virtue of placing me above everything else, of never disobeying me for anyone else's sake is obviously to do simply everything for my sake. Never placing either yourself or anyone else above me is essential; doing everything for my sake alone is perfection. The person who does everything for my sake alone does not run the risk of disobeying me for someone else's sake. This person soars far above the world and its dangers, flies straight toward me, and if done faithfully, will come as close as possible to my throne.

36. "Repay... to God what belongs to God" (Lk 20:25).

God gives us everything, so we must render everything to God. Every moment of our lives, everything we have, everything we are, must be used solely for his sake, since absolutely everything was given us by him. That is right. In his goodness, in his mercy, he allows us not to always be directly concerned with him, as long as we do not disobey him and always remain concerned with doing good.

But that is mercy on his part. Righteousness, love and perfection demand that we do absolutely everything for his sake alone: righteousness, because since we received everything from God, we must repay it all to him; love, because when we love, we are constantly concerned with our beloved and do everything for our beloved's sake; perfection, because it requires that we do everything for that purpose, and since our purpose is the glory of God, perfection is to do everything for the sake of his glory.

JOHN

37. "No one can receive anything except what has been given him from heaven" (Jn 3:27).

Everything is therefore given to us from God. And it is therefore fair to return it to him. "Repay to God what belongs to God" (Lk 20:25). And everything is God's. We owe him every moment of our lives, everything we have and our entire being. We must therefore repay to him our every moment, everything we have and everything we are, by using all of that solely for his sake, so as to most glorify him. Let us thus do everything for the sake of God alone, and let us seek solely his greater glory in everything.

38. "My food is to do the will of the one who sent me" (Jn 4:34).

To do the will of your Father, to act for his sake, was your food, what you lived on. May it also be our food, our life: to act constantly for your sake, to live on that, to live on the thought of your will, on the thought of your glory, on seeking it, fulfilling it. To focus constantly on your will and your glory. That is our life, our daily bread, our food at every moment, following your example, my Lord and God!

39. "Whoever speaks on his own seeks his own glory, but whoever seeks the glory of the one who sent him is truthful and there is no wrong in him" (Jn 7:18).

Our Lord suggests here that he constantly sought the glory of the one who sent him, that his life, his purpose, his goal were the glory of his Father. And that consequently, he sought it constantly, kept it always in sight, and that he always acted for its sake. He sought the glory of his Father, and that was his life. He did everything for the sake of that goal: his thoughts, his actions, all his movements were for the sake of God's glory.

That is the example he sets for us, the example we must follow. And we must follow that example out of love for him, because we imitate what we love. We must follow it because God's glory is our purpose, just as it was his, and the purpose of the Church, just as it is the purpose of all creation. The creatures with no conscience obtain God's glory necessarily but involuntarily; creatures with a conscience must obtain it freely and voluntarily. Let us do everything for God's sake: may all our thoughts, our words, our actions be like Jesus', for the sake of God's greater glory.

40. "I came for this hour.... Father, glorify your name" (Jn 12:27-28).

Jesus came for the hour of martyrdom, for the hour of the great sacrifice he made for God, for the hour of the holocaust that brought God the greatest glory. You came for that hour. You came to glorify God, that was your purpose. Hence you say: "Father, glorify your name." And our purpose is also to glorify God. Our purpose is to glorify him as best we can, since our duty is to love him as much as possible. Since our duty is to love him above everything else at every moment of our life, our purpose is to seek his glory above everything else at every moment of our life.

May every moment of our life therefore be used for his sake, to think, say and do what is for his greater glory. Father, glorify in us your name, in me, in those for whom I must pray most, in all people, your children, in you, by you and for you. Amen!

FAITH

MATTHEW

1. "Allow it now, for thus it is fitting for us to fulfill all righteousness" (Mt 3:15).

This means that it is thus fitting for us to fulfill what is foretold in the Scriptures. With *faith* we must believe the slightest details, follow the slightest teachings of the Holy Books, since our Lord teaches us so: "not the smallest part" of which "will pass from the law until all things have taken place" (Mt 5:18). That is the first word Saint Matthew gives us, that the Gospel gives us: we must observe the slightest teachings of the Gospel. And Saint Matthew sets the example for us.

2. "He fasted for forty days and forty nights and afterwards he was hungry" (Mt 4:2).

Was this fast a miracle or is it an example of the faith with which we must devote ourselves to penitence, counting on God — who called us there — to support us? Saint Francis of Assisi, Saint Simon Stylite and Saint Macaire all did so. It therefore seems that the fast was not a miracle, but that our Lord did it to convince us of the strengths we can find within ourselves when, by putting our faith in God, we devote ourselves with faith to the fulfillment of everything he asks of us, as impossible as it might seem.

The great, divine feat here is *faith*, trust in God, courage — and not fasting. In any case, even if the fast was a miracle, the miracle would have been an effect of *faith*, trust in God and courage, but mainly *faith*.

3. "One does not live by bread alone, but by every word that comes forth from the mouth of God" (Mt 4:4).

What faith our Lord demonstrates even in the slightest words of the Holy Scriptures! What an example he sets to believe to the letter the words of the Holy Books! And what courage, what divine wisdom, what madness in the eyes of the world he shows in practicing what he reads in the Scriptures, no matter how impossible it seems! Through this example, what theoretical and practical faith he teaches us to have for everything in the Holy Scriptures, whether it seems big or small!

4. "You shall not put the Lord, your God, to the test" (Mt 4:7).

Isaiah explains the meaning of this verse. The king of Judah was told to ask for a sign from the Lord to test the truth of the Lord's words. He answered: "I will not tempt the Lord" (Is 7:11-12). We must not test God! We must believe in him, without needing any miracle. We must not be like one of those Pharisees who asked Jesus for a sign, a miracle in heaven. We must believe in God and not ask him for proof of his words.

My God, show me the practical application of this verse, the conclusion I must draw from it for my life. Tell me, Lord, you at whose feet I lie in this sweet, blessed nighttime *tete-a-tete,* in the silence of this little house in which you have allowed me to sit at your feet. "Give your servant, therefore, an understanding heart" (1 K 3:9) for he longs to understand your Word in order to obey it.

It means, as in Isaiah: Believe the word of God, believe that I am the Son of God, believe the full truth of all my words and consequently love me, obey me, obey my slightest suggestion, my slightest desires, my slightest works, my slightest wishes, without any miracles, without any extraordinary favors, without any exceptional, miraculous grace, without understanding why, but on the simple word of the Gospel, the indications of our superiors, our directors, the secret inspirations of grace.

What Satan saw of Jesus was enough for him to know that he was the Son of God; he had no need to test God further.

What Achaz heard in the words of Isaiah was enough for him to know that they came from the Holy Spirit; he did not need to test God by asking him for a miracle. Knowing that the Gospel is the word of God is enough for us to do everything he advises, everything Jesus sets the example for. It is enough for us to know, through the Gospel, through the revelations made to the saints, through the example of the saints, that God loves nothing more than for us to obey our church directors and superiors, to submit to them perfectly. It is enough for us to know through doctrine and the example of the saints that God speaks through secret inspirations and to have the duty to be faithful to them. We do not need to test God or ask him for any further proof.

5. "When they persecute you...Rejoice and be glad" (Mt 5:11-12).

One needs faith to do that. We know. We know that to be persecuted, degraded, beaten, condemned, deprived, is to walk hand in hand with our Lord, which is the good of goods, perfect happiness, the greatest favor that can be received on earth after Baptism, the Eucharist and final perseverance.

But in daily life, how we forget it! How all these very true thoughts disappear at the slightest insult, at the slightest injustice, at the slightest wrong done to us, often even at less than that! Let us beg God to strengthen our faith so that it becomes a habit in us, a practice that we see everything with the eyes of faith and that faith reigns in our spirits and in our hearts instead of corrupt nature and worldly sayings and tastes. Oh my God, give us faith, practical faith, constant faith; may I see everything through the eyes of faith.

6. "Offer no resistance to one who is evil. When someone strikes you on your right cheek, turn the other one to him as well" (Mt 5:39).

My God, give me the faith of these words. I know that everything you say is true, but the distance is great between general knowledge and profound conviction.

Offer no resistance to evil: Offer no resistance if I am insulted, unjustly accused, arrested, imprisoned, beaten, deprived, assaulted, robbed, if my life is threatened, but turn the other cheek. I should let it be done, the way you, my divine model, offered no resistance when you were tied up, beaten, accused, stripped, lashed, berated and crucified. That's what we must do. We are lambs among wolves: lambs must be defenseless, must let themselves be shorn and killed.

We must have enough *faith* in these words to practice them. We must eliminate from our souls whatever is worldly spirit, human wisdom, and replace it with faith, with the faith that is telling us that these words are *divine*, that they are truth itself, that by following them we experience truth and good and obey God, but that by not following them, we experience error and evil, and disobey God.

7. "Give to the one who asks of you, and do not turn your back on one who wants to borrow" (Mt 5:42).

Again, we need faith to practice this. Even among religious persons, how many do? And yet that is Jesus speaking, it is eternal, infinite truth. He speaks, we listen but do not act. Our faith is not strong enough to conquer human reticence and worldly ideas. We would rather believe our petty reasoning than the word of Jesus.

His word seems "hard" to us (cf. Jn 6:60), just as his word on the Eucharist did to the unfaithful disciples of Capernaum. He speaks, and we know that he is truth, but we do not believe him because his word shocks us. We are acting like the faithless, we are hardening our hearts so as not to hear. We hear and do not understand. We have no faith. If we had faith, we would simply fulfill the word.

Jesus set the example for us: he was asked for healing upon healing, pulled, called from everywhere during his public life. He went wherever he was called, gave to whomever asked. If someone wanted to strip him of his clothes, Jesus would not prevent him from doing so but would give him every piece of them, down to the last.

The saints also set the example for us: when Saint Benedict was asked for oil, there was only one bottle left in the monastery but he ordered it to be given. The cellar-keeper disobeyed him and kept it, so Saint Benedict threw it out the window.[1] When Saint Benedict was asked for bread, he ordered some be given and was told there was none left. At dinnertime, there was bread on the table. Asked where it came from, the cellar-keeper said he had saved it for the Community. Saint Benedict took all the bread and threw it out the window.[2] Saint Stephen of Grandmont[3] ordered his monks to follow the Gospel. After his death, the land where their monastery was built was claimed by other monks and they left without swaying, taking with them the remains of their father and settling elsewhere—"Give to the one who asks of you." And Saint Francis, while still living at home, would give to whomever asked in the name of God.[4]

This "give and loan" that seems so hard to human meanness, to worldly reasoning, is perfectly clear if we consider that God is the Father of all people, and that he wants all to love each other like good brothers and sisters and to do for each other everything that a good mother wants her children to do for each other. This consideration explains everything: Brothers and sisters must give each other, must lend each other everything, at the first request.

Our Lord repeated this doctrine a thousand ways: "You are all brothers," "whatever you do for one of these least brothers of mine, you do for me," "love one another the way I loved you, to the point of giving your blood for your neighbor." Having faith is all we need. The doctrine is luminous, sparkling, bright as the sun: Let us have faith and practice giving to those who ask, since Jesus is asking, our brother, the Son of the heavenly Father is asking. Let us lend to those who wish to borrow, since it's Jesus who wants to borrow, it's our brother, the beloved child of our Father in heaven who wants to borrow.

---

[1] *Cf. S. Gregoirem* Dialogues, *Chap. 29.*
[2] *Ibid, 8.*
[3] *Stephen de Muret, founder of the Order of Grandmont (diocese of Limoges), died in 1125.*
[4] *Cf. S. Bonaventura,* Legenda Major, *Chap. 1.*

My Lord and my God, give me faith! You who help me see your will so clearly, give me enough faith to fulfill it! You know how much, in fulfilling this precept, the flesh fights against the spirit, the world against divine truth: Give me enough faith to conquer that flesh, that worldly spirit and obey you! My God, give me faith, so that I may fulfill the word you have spoken, the word that must be fulfilled, since otherwise there will be neither love for you and you are rejected, nor love for our neighbors, nor obedience, nor detachment, but only avarice, disobedience, hardness and a lack of faith and charity.

Oh, my God, your Gospel is so beautiful, bright and luminous, but it is so far from the thoughts of this age. It is true that "as high as the heavens are above the earth, so high are my thoughts above your thoughts" (Is 55:9). Give me faith, my God, so that by breaking all these offspring of Babylon that are human reasonings against the rock that is Christ, I may embrace with all my heart the divine wisdom of the Gospel, which is madness in the eyes of people, and that I may fulfill all its teachings in such a way as to most glorify you, to comfort your heart as much as possible, in you, by you and for you. Amen.

8. *"That you may be children of your heavenly Father" (Mt 5:45).*

Here is another word in which we must have true, deep, practical faith—just *faith*! *We* are all children of God: we must therefore see the beloved children of God in all people, and not just in the good, not just in the Christians, not just in the saints, but in *all* the people. They are all children of God and consequently we must show for all of them, in our thoughts, words and actions, the tender, affectionate, loving behavior that a brother shows for his brother, behavior that always remains loving, even if the brother sins, commits evil or misbehaves. Such genuine fraternity among all people, all children of God, leads to tenderness in feelings, sweetness in words and charity in actions that explain all the precepts of the Gospel concerning charity, peace and sweetness. Nothing is more natural than these precepts if all people are considered brothers and sisters, the children of the same Father. May we therefore have *faith* in our fraternity with all people.

9. "So do not worry and say, 'What are we to eat?' or 'What are we to drink?' or 'What are we to wear?'" (Mt 6:31).

To do so we also need *faith*! My God, give me the faith I need to fully accomplish this precept. Yes, everything comes to us from you. Whether I am rich or poor, young or old, surrounded by friends or strangers, everything comes to me from you alone. From you alone do I get life, health, sickness, consolation, pain, all material goods, whether abundant or in small quantities, friends, enemies, help, persecution, everything, absolutely everything comes from you. Every hair on my head is counted and not a single sparrow falls to the ground without your permission. Everything that happens is for the good of the one chosen.

Oh God, oh Father, oh Jesus, you who died on the cross for me and who called your disciples men "of little faith" (Mt 14:31) because they were thinking about the leavening of material bread, you will always give me what is good for my soul. Sometimes it will be abundance and consolation, such as now; later it will perhaps be want and suffering. But it will always be what is good for my soul, for the soul that you love, oh Father, and to which it is so easy for you to give what is useful, oh almighty Father!

We have with us, around us, a Father who loves us with an infinite love and who is all-powerful, and we worry about material things? What madness! And this Father commanded us not to worry about such things. He told us to look at the birds and the flowers and ordered us to trust him. He said to us; "But seek first the kingdom of God and his righteousness, and all these things will be given you besides" (Mt 6:33), and we still worry? What a sacrilege! What an insult to God this lack of faith in his word means!

May we therefore have the faith and the trust that piety and reason demand we have but which the world has little room for. My God, you granted me the infinite grace of removing me from the world, help me not to keep that spirit, keep that awful worldly spirit far away from me, help me live with the spirit of the Gospel, with your Spirit. And above all, give me the *faith* that will keep me from worrying about material needs, from counting on any other person or on myself to receive what is necessary for the body, but to count on you alone for and with infinite trust, abandonment, freedom of spirit, calmness, repose and faith.

10. "Seek first the kingdom of God and his righteousness, and all these things will be given you besides" (Mt 6:33).

As explained so well by Saint Theresa, this is a *pact* God makes with us. Just as a master promises his servants that in exchange for their services he will provide them with what they need, God promises us what we *really* need, that is, what is *good for the soul*—since poverty, ultimate destitution, can be excellent for the soul. In view of this solemn commitment he has made, asking him for material goods would not only be useless since he promised to give them to us in so far as he knows that it is good for us, but insulting: it would mean lacking faith in his promise and telling him we do not trust his word.

For a soul devoted to God, asking him for material bread means telling him: you took me on as your servant, you promised never to let me be in need of anything, but you are letting me go without anything, you are letting me die of hunger. You promised, but I must remind you because I'm terribly afraid you'll forget. It would be like a servant in the home of a rich, kind master going to his master every morning and begging him: Please, please don't let me die of hunger today! Such a servant would be considered crazy, as would anyone devoted to God if, after God so formally committed himself here, we still prayed to him for our material needs. We need not pray to him for anything in this respect. He promised to give us everything besides if we serve him faithfully.

There are only two things for us to do: first, serve him as

best we can, and second, not to ask him for material goods, but to thank him for them, since if we truly belong to him, we will necessarily receive such goods in so far as they are useful for our souls. It is necessary, certain, absolute. God promised us. Heaven and earth will pass, but God's word will not. My God, give me *faith* in your word. It is clear we must have it, but how many do? Give it to me, my God, in you, by you and for you!

11. "The measure with which you judge others will be measured out to you" (Mt 7:2).

My God, give me true faith in this word. There is such a difference between knowing about it, grasping it and believing it in practice! You added these words after "Stop judging, that you may not be judged." Thus, we must give others what we want to receive from God not only in action and words, but also in thoughts. For harsh judgments, we will receive a harsh judgment, for cold or hard words we will receive cold or hard words, for hurtful actions, we will receive a hurtful punishment.

If we really believed this, how our lives would change! How all people would be real brothers and sisters! How we would be everything to everyone! How we would practice the Gospel, giving to everyone, not refusing anything, allowing anything to be done to us, doing for others what we would have God do for us! What a guideline for life in these words! What does genuine faith in these words not comprise? To love others as we want to be loved by God; to comfort others as we would like God to comfort us the day we appear before him; to work toward the sanctification of others as we want God to work toward ours; to seek the salvation of others when they need it, when they ask for it, as we want God to give us ours when we need it, when we ask for it; to forgive as we want God to forgive us; to be tender and loving, as we want God to be tender and loving to us.

What charity! What tender thoughts, words and actions! What a life of universal love! And this is not a dream, it is what God, what unfailing truth, eternal wisdom, specifically command us. This is not something we could doubt, this is God speaking. His words are infinitely clear, he has repeated them in several passages and restated them in several ways: "The measure with which you judge others will be measured out to you."

Oh, my God, give me faith, true faith, practical faith, the faith that makes the Gospel part of life, the faith of someone building on solid rock and not the dead faith of someone building on sand. My God, give me faith, the faith that helps me meditate on your words to understand them and then practice them for the rest of my life, the faith that creates the life of the righteous because it bases life on new foundations,[5] quite different from those of all other people, who consider them madness: "As high as the heavens above the earth, so high...are my thoughts above your thoughts" (Is 55:9).

12. "Courage, daughter! Your faith has saved you" (Mt 9:22).

Our Lord praised the faith of this woman who had touched the tassel on his cloak. She believed in his goodness and she went to him without hesitating. Whenever we go to him that way, without hesitating, our prayers will be granted, unless of course we ask for something harmful or not as good as what he wants to give. In that case, in his goodness, he has the prerogative of correcting the petition and of giving instead what would have been petitioned if the person had been more enlightened, what is best instead of something less good or evil.

Which would be better, asking God for this or for that? Or should we simply pray to him: Give me what would most glorify you? Let us pray as God inspires us: both ways are good, when carried out with absolute *faith* in his power and in his goodness, with absolute *faith* that our prayers will be granted if what we pray for is truly good for us. However,

---

[5]Fides est humanae salutis initium fundamentum et redix omnis justificationis. *Council of Trent, Sess. VI, Chap. VIII.*

when praying for something specific, we should add out loud, or at least in our heart, "yet not as I will, but as you will..." (Mt 26:39). Both types of prayer are good. We must say the one that we feel most attracted to, and we should not consider the second inferior to the first: it implies just as much faith in God, but less faith in ourselves, less self-confidence in our own judgment. It means we do not trust ourselves to know what is truly good, what we should pray for, and therefore leave the choice up to God, praying to him trustfully: Give us what will most glorify you. I don't know what that is, but you do.

13. "Let it be done to you according to your faith" (Mt 9:29).

Our Lord linked healing to the *faith* of those requesting it. He granted their request in accordance with the *faith* with which it was made. Faith is not exactly the certainty of receiving what has been requested, but the certainty of the power and infinite, divine goodness of Jesus, who can heal us and who will probably do it if we ask him to. But if it is bad for us, or if he wants to replace a request with another, better one, he will do so. In short, the faith that will get our prayers answered *is the faith that we will receive from the Almighty, either what we ask of him or something better.* Thus we must believe strongly when we pray, and then we can be certain of our prayers being granted. The word of Jesus and the goodness of God provide us with the most absolute certainty.

Let us therefore pray, let us therefore pray and pray and pray, since our prayers are so powerful, since they are arrows that never turn back, since each prayer, each word, each moment can and does obtain, if we have faith, countless graces for our neighbors and for ourselves.

14. "And he did not work many mighty deeds there because of their lack of faith" (Mt 13:58).

The people of Nazareth, while asking Jesus for miracles,

did not believe that he could work them, they had no faith in his power. That is why he did not work any miracles there.

Let us therefore have faith in his power and in his goodness and let us pray with trust. Our prayers will be answered, or else we will receive something even better. Jesus promised such a reward a hundred times for whomever prayed to him with faith. Such faith and trust honors him, pleases him. We owe it to him for a thousand reasons, and first of all, out of gratitude. Faithlessness is an insult to him, it is a refusal to acknowledge his perfections, his goodness, it means denying him what he has, it is ungratefulness, it is doubting his word.

15. "O you of little faith, why did you doubt?" (Mt 14:31).

Our Lord admonished Saint Peter for his lack of faith. Our Lord told him "Come [walk on water]" (Mt 14:29), and Saint Peter was afraid of sinking. He had started off right, with great faith, but in the face of danger, his faith wobbled. He was entirely wrong, but who could throw the first stone at him? Who, except Jesus, has the right to condemn him for what unfortunately so many souls do? He was wrong, entirely wrong, since Jesus had called him and consequently necessarily given him all the graces to go to him; in so far as he had said "Come [walk on water]," Jesus had given Saint Peter the necessary grace to do so. To doubt, to lack faith after such a categorical calling is a definite sin. It means lacking faith in the goodness, in the righteousness and in the truthfulness of God.

It's also a sin that I unfortunately commit often, my God! How many times have I told myself "I can't do it" regarding something good, something you wanted, since I had permission to do it and it seemed good to me. Forgive me, my God, for all this lack of faith! Give me perfect faith in the future, let me see clearly in everything. And if you want me to do it, and as soon as I am aware of it, as soon as I know that you have said to me "Come," let me jump onto the water like my dear Saint Peter and walk on the water to the end, with the absolute faith that by your call of "Come," you have given me everything I need to go to you, to follow you, to accompany you, to do whatever you ask.

16. "O woman, great is your faith! Let it be done for you as you wish" (Mt 15:28).

Let us pray with faith, with faith in the power and goodness of God the infinitely powerful and the infinitely good, with faith in the infinitely truthful promise of God, who tells us so often "anything for which they are to pray, it shall be granted to them by my heavenly Father" (Mt 18:19) and "If you have faith the size of a mustard seed, you will say to this mountain, 'Move from here to there,' and it will move" (Mt 17:19). We *must* believe that God answers all the prayers that we say to him with faith. He answers them in two ways, either by granting what we ask for or by granting us something better. Thus, when we pray to him, we can either ask for something specific, although always adding "yet not as I will, but as you will" (Mt 26:39), or else not ask for anything in particular, but simply say "Please give me what will most comfort you, what will most glorify you."

17. "An evil and unfaithful generation seeks a sign" (Mt 16:4).

Our Lord scorned the Pharisees for their lack of faith, not that we must believe anything without examining it first, not that we must believe anything without proof: our faith must be based on reason, as Saint Paul said. But once we have been given adequate evidence, we must believe: not to believe after seeing adequate evidence is bad faith. Such bad faith was how the Pharisees sinned, and that is how so many others sin by closing their eyes so they cannot see.

Save me, my God, from that bad faith, from that stubbornness, from that hardening, and make me always believe everything that you want me to believe, through whatever sign, through whatever proof, through whatever voice you teach me!

In addition to what the Holy Church teaches me, I must thus receive from you the words of my director, the events which guide my life and teach me your will for me, the advice of your Holy Gospels, attractions, good thoughts and good examples, everything you use to lead me. I must act carefully in everything out of love and not out of lack of faith, to be sure to do your will, so dear to me, and which is "what I love."

But in everything, as soon as I see the necessary proof of your will—and I must seek it avidly, passionately, lovingly, without waiting for it—I must believe and carry out that blessed will without asking for new signs. The necessary, sufficient sign for me will be my director's word, not that his word is the only sign, but all the others must be related to him, and it is up to him to judge their value, their meaning and their origin.

18. *"You of little faith, why do you conclude among yourselves that it is because you have no bread" (Mt 16:8).*

Jesus rebuked them for being worried and fearful. We must work to live, but without worrying about whether our work will give us bread. And anyway, our work will not give us our bread, God will, and God alone. Our hairs are counted; whatever happens to us, happens by his will. If we receive bread, he gave it to us. If we can't get any, he wants us to fast for our own good.

Let us do our duty, let us allot so many hours a day to work, so many hours to prayer, to prayer alone outside of any other occupation, since we must constantly pray while working, while walking, while talking, and in doing so we must not worry at all about where our bread will come from.

Jesus said "Seek first the kingdom of God and his righteousness, and all this will be given you besides" (Mt 6:33). Let us do good, let us do what is most perfect, let us carry out God's will and expect from God the food he promised so clearly to whomever seeks his kingdom. Let us expect it with absolute faith that however we receive it, God gave it to us, and that whatever quantity of it we receive, it is the amount intended by God himself and is particularly useful for our souls.

19. "If you have faith the size of a mustard seed, you will say to this mountain, 'Move from here to there,' and it will move" (Mt 17:19).

Making a mountain move from here to there is as easy for God as healing the sick or doing any other work. If, quieting our human thoughts, we ask him for something with good, pure intentions, he will grant it to us, or else he will give us something better. If we ask him with faith, with absolute faith in God's power and goodness, in his present words, we will receive what we asked for or something better. That is the principle of miracles, a dual principle: God's word cannot not be fulfilled, and the conditions imposed by his word, human faith, mean the firm belief that we will receive either what we pray for or something better.

20. "If you have faith and...say to this mountain, 'Be lifted up and thrown into the sea,' it will be done. Whatever you ask for in prayer with faith, you will receive" (Mt 21:21-22).

As you tell us repeatedly, my God, that prayer is all-powerful, that we must pray and pray and pray, because our prayers, if faithful, will always be answered, always, even when we don't realize it. Sometimes we don't realize it and think our prayers haven't been answered when actually they have been answered beyond our expectations. We continue to pray, when we have already received something greater than what we asked for: God, in his greatness, substituted a greater gift for a smaller one. For example, someone may pray for physical health for a loved one, and that person receives a sound soul too; someone else might ask for temporal favors such as relief from passing ills, and instead receive spiritual graces and deliverance from the evils of purgatory.

If we pray *with faith* we will always receive either what we ask for or something better. That is, the faith we must have: that almighty, infinitely good God answers all the prayers we say with faith, and he does so by virtue of his goodness and truthfulness because he promised us to; and that he answers them either by giving us what we ask for or by giving us something better.

Oh, if we really had faith in that word! How we would pray! How we would ask! My God, give me that faith, let me participate as you allow me not only in your almighty power but also in your infinite wisdom. Yes, truly your infinite wisdom, since my prayers will always include these words, either spoken or understood: "Yet not my will but yours" (Mt 26:39). I am therefore praying for your will itself, for what your wisdom itself wants, and my prayers are thus infinitely wise and all powerful, they are truly a divine act.

Oh, my God, may I repeat them as often as possible, since they bring me so close to you, since they are a source of such good for my brothers and sisters that I must love dearly for your sake, since they unite me so strongly with you by transforming my will into your will and your will into mine, by transforming my words into your action. How prayer joins me with you! If it is a blessing for others what a blessing it is for me, through this intimate bond it establishes between you and me.

Oh, my God, for your glory, I ask you with faith and in the name of Jesus, give me faith and may I pray as much as you want me to and the way you want me to. To start with, I have two things to ask you: Forgive me for my faithlessness yesterday and today, and especially for my sad error of not having kept your presence enough, of not having said my prayers carefully enough and of not having gotten up as soon as I was awakened by you.

Forgive me, please, my heavenly Father, forgive me, my Jesus! And help me, in the name of God, not to slip back into my sins today or tomorrow. Help me be faithful to you on this day, help me comfort your heart, oh, my Jesus. I boldly ask this of you, oh Jesus, I pray to you with faith, because you love me and it is easy for you to do anything: Do not let me commit any imperfections during this 24-hour period. And I have something else to ask of you, since both your goodness and your power are boundless: Do not let me commit any sin throughout my entire life.

In truth, it is a dogma that everyone, except the Blessed Virgin, commits venial sins, but I have sinned enough in the past to have filled my quota, and since you are good and infinitely powerful, I am praying to you, knowing that you will grant my prayers or give me something better, since, to improve my virtues, it is perhaps better for you to let me occasionally stoop to imperfections in order to sense my affliction. Again I ask this of you, my God, saying: "Yet not my will, but your will" (Mt 26:39).

But there is something I want to ask of you above all, my Father, my Jesus, and that I am asking with faith, that is to let me comfort you as much as possible at every moment of my life. And what I am asking for myself, my God, I am asking for all your children: that all people comfort you as much as possible throughout their lives. Amen. Amen. Amen.

21. "Sky and earth will pass away but my words will never pass away" (Mt 24:35).

Your words, my God, are divine. They are eternal truth. They are both infinitely true and infinitely perfect. We must therefore first of all believe them with invincible confidence; secondly, we must follow them with scrupulous fidelity; third, we must carefully study them, since you deigned to utter them for us; and fourth, we must direct all our energy to understanding their meaning.

1) To believe them, that is evident; it would be madness and frightening impiety not to believe when God speaks;

2) We must follow them, since they are the truth, perfection, the will of God; it is evident that goodness, perfection, duty and the love of God require us to follow them without restraint. Our life, our aspiration, our need, our only repose and our only happiness must be for us to model ourselves on perfection and at all times on the words of our beloved, our Savior, our everything, our God. His words must govern all our thoughts, all our words, all our actions, all the moments of our life. This is what our duty is; this is what love is;

3) We must study the divine words, those which Jesus spoke from his human mouth and which were quoted by the evangelists and apostles, as well as those spoken by the Holy Spirit in the other Holy Books, but especially the Gospel which contains the summary of everything, which repeats everything, which explains everything.

But all of the Scriptures contain infinite treasures. One must love them, adore them and cherish them entirely, read and reread them with great care, great zeal, great love, reading them to follow them because they are God's words, reading them to follow them, because we cannot make them our rule if we do not know them well, reading them to imitate Jesus who undoubtedly read them and who knew them well, often quoting them and saying: "All this happened to fulfill the prophecies in Scripture" (cf. Mt 26:56; 27:9; Mk 14:26; Lk 22:37; Jn 19:24; 19:28). Let us therefore regularly spend time reading them, and study them well, first of all to follow them and secondly to imitate our beloved and respect his words;

4) We must try to understand God's words. It is our duty to do so in order to imitate Jesus, out of respect, but especially in order to follow the divine word in practice. This requires for us, first of all, to pray to God for this understanding to the extent that it is useful for the glory of God; secondly, to assiduously meditate on the Holy Scriptures; third, to read the books of Catholic doctors who comment on them, not just any books but books with a very reliable doctrine, books by great souls and great saints, such as Saint Augustine, Saint John Chrysostom and Saint Thomas of Aquinas. Equal care should be taken to researching the books by great saintly writers and to avoid those by lower, less perfect ones.

In addition to the commentaries themselves, we should also read all the books about religious perfection written by great, saintly doctors, since all these books, regardless of their titles, are but commentaries on the Gospel. We might add the lives of saints, especially those written by saints, the very brief ones which contain only facts. The lives of saints are also a sort of commentary on the Gospel, less reliable than the others since while the saints were perfect in their faithfulness to grace, they didn't always have the clear-sightedness which makes one clearly see the truth. But there are always very good teachings to be learned from them and the Holy Spirit who guided them did not let them err in important matters. The Church, which canonized them, judged all the examples which they left, modeled on the Holy Gospel, and it was because they acted as models that they were canonized. Let us perfect our knowledge of the Holy Books by reading about the actions and writings of saints, and let us in particular study the writings of great doctors, and those whom the Church recognizes as great lights.

22. *"Insofar as you did this to one of the least of these brothers of mine, you did it to me" (Mt 25:40).*

Let us have faith in these words and our life will be transformed. There are perhaps no words in the Gospel so capable of changing our existence. They make us see everything in a new light, and what a light! People then aren't just our brothers and sisters, they are Jesus himself. We should no longer do unto them as we would wish done unto us, nor what we would do for our brothers and sisters, but what we would do for Jesus. Everything we do for them, we do for Jesus.

If we really have faith in this, in these words, in these words of God, eternal truth, what love there would be in our hearts, what feelings of tenderness for all human beings! We would see Jesus in everyone, divine Jesus, the infinitely loveable, the good master, the crucified Savior. What feelings in our souls! What a change deep in our hearts! And what a change in our spiritual life! What prayers for these people who are Jesus! What wishes for their health, their saintliness, their eternal happiness, their perfection! What zeal for these souls who are the soul of Jesus! What efforts to sanctify them to the utmost, to do them the best possible good! The good we do them is an eternal good done to Jesus! What apostolic spirit, what burning zeal these words fill our souls with!

And what a change in our material life! All the poor, needy and afflicted, all the suffering are Jesus! What deeds of charity! "To give alms," said the Abbot de Rance,[6] "there is no need to establish rules, it is only necessary to have faith, to believe that the poor are Jesus and act accordingly." How we would end up depriving ourselves of everything, and becoming impoverished in order to give to Jesus the poor one! What charity! What alms and consequently, what poverty!

Love for our neighbor, zealous souls, prayers, apostolic works, charitable works, evangelical poverty, these are the results to which faith in these words immediately leads. They are not the only ones, since holy poverty brings with it a multitude of virtues: humility, penitence, solitude, abjection, manual labor, often obedience and especially often chastity. Poverty necessarily provides all of that or usually leads to it, and in any event always helps.

What a transformation in life! This word alone is enough for us, if we receive it with faith, to place ourselves into burning charity and absolute poverty. My God, as you know, you have already done me much good with these words. Make me receive them with increasingly intense faith and make them entirely transform my soul, my heart, my inner life, my outer life and make me become what you want me to be. Amen.

23. "Insofar as you neglected to do this to one of the least of these, you neglected to do it to me" (Mt 25:45).

What solemn words, and how they complete the preceding ones! If we received these words with faith, how we would painfully look inside ourselves and see that it is absolutely necessary for us to change our lives entirely. We must no longer live for ourselves but for our neighbor, who is Jesus. We must forget about ourselves, which is the first thing that Jesus wants from his disciples. Not only must we do good to others at certain times, but we must never let a chance to do good to a neighbor pass by without acting on it.

---

[6] *Armand de Rance, founder of the Trappe, died 1700.*

Neglect is serious for it is Jesus whom we neglect to save! It is not enough to give to those who ask, we must give to those who need. Every time we do not give spiritual or material aid to someone who needs it, it is Jesus whom we are neglecting to help! We must organize our lives according to our calling, in order to do the best possible good to all those within reach of our spiritual and temporal action, in order to not commit this terrible, painful neglect of Jesus. And we must try with all the means within our power to extend this spiritual and material action as far as possible, to help Jesus as much as possible, to reach him as far as possible, to comfort him to the greatest extent, in as many beings as possible.

We can accomplish this twofold action marvelously through prayer, through prayer said with faith, in which we avail ourselves of the spiritual and temporal wealth of our heavenly Father. We should also always include penitence, which in one aspect is like prayer, as well as setting the example. For those whom God calls to a life completely apart from the world, as hermits living in absolute solitude, that is sufficient; for others, it is not enough. Each person, according to one's calling, must add to these three things everything afforded by the condition in which God has willed him or her, considering that neighbors are Jesus, and that the help given to them is given to Jesus, and that all beings he or she neglects to help is Jesus. It is therefore clear that every time a moral or physical good is possible and compatible with our calling, it must be done and, if we love Jesus and if we have faith in his words, we must organize our lives in order to do the best possible good, spiritually and temporally, to the greatest possible number of people.

24. *"This is my body...this is my blood" (Mt 26:26-28).*

Oh my God, if I had as much faith as I should, and I do have faith in these words—there is nothing in the world of which I am more certain—but if *in practice* I had the faith I should have, if this faith illuminated my soul with a bright enough light, what happiness and fervor I would have in attending mass, expositions and blessings of the Blessed Sacrament, in receiving the Holy Communion, at the foot of the tabernacle, in church! What fervor would replace my present lack of enthusiasm! What love, what happiness, what desire to be at the altar as much as possible, to never willingly lose a single moment of presence in church!

Jesus is in church as present as he was at the cenacle, at Nazareth, in Bethany, in Bethlehem, in Gethsemane, at the crucifixion. He tells me to love him with the most ardent love. He is there, I can go near him, he allows me, he calls me and I don't go, I go slowly, I only go half the time I could go! What indignity! Jesus, my beloved master, do not let me do that anymore. It is too ungrateful, too indifferent, too indignant and spiteful! Our Lady of Perpetual Help, rescue me from such a horrible sin! My father Saint Joseph, to whom I particularly entrusted the keeping of myself in our Lord's company, help me! My mother Saint Magdalene, my guardian angel, save me!

25. *"Or do you think that I cannot appeal to my Father, who would promptly send more than twelve legions of angels to my defense?" (Mt 26:53).*

Oh yes! If we had faith, we would fear no danger, we would not resist evil since Jesus said: "Offer no resistance to the wicked" (Mt 5:39). Instead, we would see everyone, our enemies, our persecutors, as instruments of God accomplishing his work in us. We would be absolutely sure that if it was not better for our souls for us to suffer these things, he who told us, "Do not resist," "I am sending you out like sheep among wolves" (Mt 10:16), "If anyone hits you on the right cheek, offer him the other as well; if someone wishes to go to law with you to get your tunic, let him have your cloak as well" (Mt 5:40), he who loved us enough to have himself nailed to the cross for us and who commands all the legions of angels, and without whose will not a hair would fall from our head, would certainly deliver us.

Our good angel is always there, Jesus is always there: What they allow, let us allow. They do not expect us to struggle against people in order to take ourselves out of poverty, suffering or death, but rather to accept and lovingly offer destitution, suffering and death for the love of Jesus, for the sake of his greatest glory, out of obedience and imitation, in the spirit of victims offering themselves, of children accepting everything from their father as they embrace him, with the tender gratitude of a wife who knows that her husband can do her no greater favor than to share his suffering with her, who melts in gratitude when seeing that he deigns to involve her, to have her walk in his footsteps and make her resemble him so much.

26. "He offered not a word in answer to any of the charges" (Mt 27:14).

If we really had faith in these words, if we viewed Jesus' silence before Pilate with faith, how could we open our mouths to defend ourselves, to excuse ourselves? How could we wish to be respected by others, how could we fear humiliation and disgrace? How could we not wish to be scorned, disdained and heaped with insults? I say: If we had faith, because with the little faith we have, wisdom tells us to imitate infinite perfection in all its examples and consequently to remain silent before accusations. (Was there ever a more just cause to defend oneself, either for the saintliness of the accused, or for the seriousness of the evil to avoid?), and love tells us to desire, to seek resemblance with our beloved, by sharing his crown of thorns, his humiliations, his disgrace. Lord Jesus, give me this faith, this wisdom, this love. Give me the blessing of following your example, of being like you, silent when accused, unless the benefit of souls requires some words, as you showed me, and give me the blessing of sharing your humiliations and disgrace with love and happiness. I deserve them, you suffered them without deserving them and to what excess, for the love of me! My God, let this faith change and transform my life!

27. *"And they stripped him..." (Mt 27:28).*

My God, give me faith in these words, true faith, not the kind of faith which believes this and then no longer thinks about it, which accepts it as a historic truth and goes no further, not a dead and paralyzed faith but a living, urgent, active faith. If we truly believe this as we should believe it, how our lives would be transformed! What pain at the core of our souls, what love of the cross! How we would suffer when thinking about the sufferings of our beloved! How we would embrace mortification! What an ardent desire we would have, in order to resemble our spouse, to be crowned with his crown, to share his fate, to have our bodies bloody and mangled like his, to have our souls in anguish and bodies in the final throes of pain so as not to be treated better than you, to follow you in all your paths, to walk in your footsteps, to be like you, my beloved Jesus. You whom I love with all my heart, all my strength, all my soul, all my mind, you to whom I give my heart and my life, you from whom I want your will and nothing but your will. My God, you who are always with me, you who cover me with your shadow, you who are in me and around me, with the power to do everything and govern all things, make me do what is most perfect, what glorifies you the most, that is all I want and all I ask for. Lord Jesus, hallowed be your name. Amen. Amen. Amen.

28. *"And they spat on him and took the reed and struck him on the head with it..." (Mt 27:30).*

Oh my Lord Jesus, who are present here, who allow me to be at your feet during these silent hours of the night, who invited me here, wishing to have me miserable and unworthy before you, thinking of you, looking at you, speaking to you, listening to you, in a *tete-a-tete* for several hours with you, while all is at rest and while so many other souls are asleep! Oh my God, how good you are! What have I done to deserve such happiness? What have I done to receive from you this call of predilection, this blessed invitation? My Jesus, how happy I am! Thank you! Thank you! And thank you for having awakened me.

You called me, you awakened me, you made me rise, and you caused the depths of my heart to feel the sweetness of my fate; what a good experience, what a loving experience you have given me! And now you tell me to think about your passion and to understand once and for all that if I really had the faith that I should have, together with a little bit of love, there would be no disgrace, humiliation, mockery, mistreatment or persecution which I would not receive with joy, which I would not desire, which I would not seek, which I would not bear with courage, patience and love, which I would not love, because all of them would make me closer to my beloved.

They would make me beautiful with his beauty, crowning me with his diadem, making me share his fate, making me walk in his footsteps, hand in hand, bearing his cross, comforting him, entering in his work, helping in his work, giving him a sign of love, suffering because of him and for him, heightening his glory, comforting his heart and at the same time increasing my love for him in time, my knowledge and my love for him in eternity. "Blessed are you when people abuse and persecute you...Rejoice and be glad" (Mt 5:11), said the divine Savior in the beatitudes. Oh yes! With what joy, what zeal, what desire, what love must I embrace disgrace and mistreatment if I believe in the Gospel and if I love you, Lord Jesus, my beloved spouse! Give me this blessing!

29. *"They gave him wine to drink mixed with gall, which he tasted but refused to drink" (Mt 27:34).*

My God, if we had faith in these words, if we really believed in this act, if we really saw you at such a time suffering such torture, refusing the drink which would numb your senses and slightly diminish your suffering, how could we, whose sufferings are so slight compared to yours and so deserved, ever ask for, ever wish for the slightest comfort and relief? Imitating you, wishing to act as you do, is enough for those who have faith never to seek to lighten the suffering which God offers them. Further there are also all the motives which you yourself had and even more: the will to not diminish the sacrifice of enduring pain which, the greater it was, the more it glorified your Father. You had the will to declare your love to God through the greatest pain suffered for him, the will to declare your love to people through the greatest pain suffered for them, the will to leave this example for people; and furthermore you had the will to not refuse from the hand of Jesus our brother, the favor he did for us by offering to let us suffer with him, the will to grow closer to God, and that of detaching ourselves from earth, the will of imitating Jesus, and that of helping him with Simon of Cyrene carry the cross, the will of expiating for our sins.

But above all, his example is our path, his example was given to us for us to follow, his example is the most perfect, what pleases him most, what his Father wanted from him and wants from us. If we have faith, we should follow this example out of love, because love lives of resemblance. The resemblance is the beginning of conformity, the beginning of union; union, unity, to "be so perfected in unity" (Jn 17:23), is what love by its nature tends to bring about. Through wisdom we must also follow this example, because the example of Jesus is perfection itself.

30. "Jesus again crying out in a loud voice, yielded up his spirit" (Mt 27:50).

If we had faith in these words, if we believed as we should that Jesus died for us, how we would love him and how we would wish for martyrdom! We would love him. Suppose that an ugly, unintelligent person, of the lowest class, rejected in every way by all human creatures, voluntarily died for love of us. Would we not love that person? Nothing attracts love more than love: it is likely that we could not help giving our heart to this poor being who loved us so passionately. And we would refuse it to Jesus! There is no being so unworthy that we would not love him or her if that person loved us that much: Jesus gives us proof of love: He is supreme beauty, infinite goodness, intelligence, knowledge, perfect wisdom, eternal truth, he is God. How could we not love him?

Into what abyss my heart has plunged! To what depths of

misery I have fallen! In what deep mire I am buried! My God, who died for me, I am at your feet, I adore you with all the strength of my soul, I love you, I want to love you, I ask to love you with all my heart. Thank you, thank you for having died for unworthy me! Forgive me for having loved you so little. Help me so that I can love you as I should, as you want me to!

If we have faith, we must also ardently wish for martyrdom, since it would mean resembling Jesus to the end, being his brother, his little brother to the end, following him hand in hand to the Cross. That would be giving him the greatest sign of love. "No one can have greater love than to lay down his life for his friends" (Jn 15:13).

31. "Go, therefore, make disciples of all nations, baptize them..." (Mt 28:19).

If we really had faith in these words, what apostolic spirit we would have! What zeal in our souls! These were the last words of Jesus to his apostles: he thus set out their mission on earth, their whole lives' work. It is the complement, the commentary, the application of the supreme commandment: "Love one another" (Jn 15:12). It is the method, the manner in which they must practice this commandment. It means practicing the first two commandments, the love of God and love of neighbor.

The way for the apostles to practice these commandments is to convert souls. They can do nothing which would glorify God more, nor which would do more good to their fellow beings: conversion, the sanctification of souls, contains the zeal of the glory of God and the zeal of souls. It is the most we can do here on earth, for both the love of God and the love of our fellow beings. That was the purpose of Jesus' life on earth. "The Son of man came not to be served but to serve, and to give his life as a ransom for many" (Mt 20:28). It is the purpose of the Church, the purpose of each soul.

Loving God above all, and then loving your neighbor as yourself in the eyes of God, are what should be at the depths of our soul: to love is to seek the good of what he loves. Our first fruit is to seek the good of God, that is, God's glory; our second is to seek the good of our neighbors, that is, their sanctification. The only glory of God that we can obtain is the external manifestation of his glory, which consists of people's love and praise, in other words, the sanctification of all people, for the sake of God's glory. That is our goal; that is the goal which Jesus proposed to all his disciples when he ascended to heaven. That was what he wanted them to devote the rest of their time on earth to. Everybody, men and women, apostles and every single disciple, have this same goal: it is the work of all of them, since it is the necessary result of the twofold love which is our greatest duty. It is everyone's goal since they all share the same goal as Jesus, their leader, and the Church, their mother.

We must therefore devote ourselves to the sanctification of all people, ourselves and our fellow beings, for the sake of God's glory and all the more completely, solely for the glory of God, that we wish to live completely, uniquely for the glory of God, to accomplish his will, for his love. Whether we have been called to active life or live hidden like Jesus at Nazareth this should be the purpose of our every moment, our every thought, our every word and action. If we want all our moments, thoughts, words and actions to be used for the glory of God, then our desires, our prayers, our requests, our words, our mortification and works must be consequently directed toward this goal.

The sanctification of all people means our own and that of others: Our own, first of all, because it is our special duty; secondly, because we have a great deal more blessings, strength and means to obtain it; and third, because we cannot work effectively on the sanctification of others until we have acquired our own to a sufficient degree. My God, give us faith in those last words you pronounced on earth, and which are the practical means to accomplish your supreme commandment of mutual love and the great twofold duty of our life of loving God and our neighbor for the sake of God. And let us organize our lives toward this goal, in accordance with you. This is the real way to imitate you: to have the same goal as you and take the same measures to obtain it; to have the same sentiments, the same great twofold love, the same purpose, the sanctification of all souls, the same goals, the imitation of your life. Saint Francis of Assisi, whom we celebrate today, you who so wonderfully understood this and practiced it so well, who was so true to Jesus in your heart, who were given a purpose to your life and the means to achieve this purpose, help me follow Jesus, but to follow him in everything, and give me the means to succeed in all moments of my life, in all my thoughts, words and actions. Hallowed be his name, his kingdom come, his will be done in me and in all present and future souls. I ask for this with you and with your intercession, oh beloved Saint Francis, in the name of our divine Master Jesus. Amen.

MARK

32. "Seeing their faith, Jesus said to the paralytic, 'My child, your sins are forgiven' " (Mk 2:5).

In this example, Jesus shows us what *faith* we must have in him, in his goodness, in his power, in what he can do when asked, in what he will certainly do if it is good for us. At the same time he shows us that if he answers prayers made with this *faith*, he does not always answer them in the way we asked but rather in the way that most benefits us, by rectifying them for our greatest benefit, by giving us either what we ask for or even more. This is the case here: the Savior was asked merely for physical health and he answered the prayer because of the faith with which it was asked. But he answered it by giving not physical health but something infinitely more valuable—spiritual health.

33. "Why are you so frightened? Have you still no faith?" (Mk 4:40).

Jesus blamed the apostles' lack of *faith* for their fright. Fear of God is the beginning of wisdom, uniting here on earth with Holy Hope. Its reverential aspects live on eternally even among angels and saints. But the fear of anything else stems from lack of faith. "Not one [sparrow] falls to the ground without your father knowing. Why every hair on your head has been counted" (Mt 10:29-30), and "We are well aware that God works with those who love him, those who have been called in accordance with his purpose, and turns everything to their good" (Rm 8:28). What is there left to fear? Nothing, absolutely nothing, except God, except displeasing him, offending him, not loving him enough, not following his will in everything we do. This is the only fear compatible with faith. The rest, whatever it may be, be it nakedness, hunger or the sword, should not frighten us because God allows them, since it is for our good, since it is only a means of sanctification offered by the hand of God. In what we call danger, need, suffering or difficulty we must pray, but with faith, that whatever happens will be for our own good, in accordance with God's will, whatever it may be, always adding out loud in our minds: "Nevertheless, let it be as you, not I, would have it" (Mt 26:39). And when we say that we *must* pray, that in no way means that we *must* ask for certain things. It means that we *must* more than ever lift our souls to God, unite with him through prayer, look at him and talk to him, since one of the purposes of danger, need and suffering, one of the reasons he allows them, is because they further unite us with God, they actively make us turn toward him, to forget the earth and look toward heaven.

He therefore wants us to raise our eyes toward him under these circumstances, but he allows us to pray in two ways. We can, like our Lord at Gethsemane, let nature speak and ask God to deliver us from suffering, danger or need, but in that case we must add immediately, as our Lord did, "Nevertheless, let it be as you, not I, would have it." Or we could, silencing nature and letting only our faith and love of God speak, simply cry out: "Our Father in heaven, may your name be held holy" (Mt 6:9), make anything happen as long as it is for your greatest glory. Do what you want with me, I only ask you for one thing, glorify your name to the utmost! Both prayers are good; God gives us the example of both. We must say one or the other according to our instincts, according to how they appeal to us. The Holy Spirit gives us an inclination toward one or the other; we only need to follow this inclination. We should also consider that when we are in need, difficulty, danger or sorrow, Jesus is always with us, he is present invisibly as he was visibly present in Peter's boat.

Under the watch and hand of this good Master, it is as impossible for us to perish spiritually (if we do not voluntarily detach ourselves from him, by rejecting his love, by refusing to obey him, by leaving his boat) as it was for the apostles to perish physically by having him with them. Our Lord blamed the apostles for two things: their fear and their lack of faith.

They could still pray to him, but pray without fear, because we should only fear one thing—offending God, for God to be offended. And it was not necessary to wake him because he is always watching. Regardless of whether he appears to be sleeping or his action seems dormant, his heart constantly watches over us and whatever happens, it will be for his glory and our good. We must have faith in this continuous surveillance by Jesus, however invisible it may be, however dormant it may appear, and we must *believe* that whatever happens will only happen with his permission and for his glory and our good.

34. *"My daughter, your faith has restored you to health; go in peace and be free of your complaint" (Mk 5:34).*

Our Lord gave faith to the hemorrhaging woman and said he granted it because of this faith. Faith in his power, faith in his goodness, let us therefore ask him for this double faith with the confidence that it will be granted and it will. But let us still say, like Jesus: "Nevertheless, let it be as you, not I, would have it," not what appears to be for my good, but what glorifies you the most. What I desire, what I ask for above all is your greatest glory, my God. And let us remember that God, in granting our wishes, perhaps gives us not what we ask for but something better—what we would ask for if we were more knowledgeable, if we had a better knowledge of our needs, and what would truly benefit us.

35. *"Do not be afraid; only have faith" (Mk 5:36).*

My Lord Jesus, here I am at your feet; unfortunately I am very late! Is a love that has such concern for these miserable bodies of ours very ardent? My Lord, guide me, lead me, make me carry out your will in everything! You know that is all I want, make me do it, my God! How blind I am! Lead me in this darkness! I do not ask you for light for the sake of light, nor more light than you want me to have. Give me what you want, but make me love you, make me comfort your heart, make this poor little creature created by your hands give you all the comfort possible, all you want from him, my Lord and my God, my beloved Jesus! It seems to me that you answer me with the words you told me to meditate upon today and which I ask you to explain to me: "Do not be afraid; only have faith." Yes, regardless of external problems, sadness, darkness, inner problems, do not fear, just believe. Do not fear, I am with you, in you, around you. I love you and am all powerful, all your hairs are counted, nothing happens to you inside or outside without my permission, and anything that happens to you is for your greatest good. You have the blessing to derive saintliness for yourself from everything, glory and comfort for myself. Do not be afraid, only have faith: I am here, I am all powerful and I love you.

36. *"For saying this you may go home happy; the devil has gone out of your daughter" (Mk 7:29).*

To reward the Sycrophenician for her faith, Jesus cured her daughter. The Sycrophenician believed in the power of Jesus and in his goodness. She also prayed to him, despite discouragement, despite the silence of the Master, despite his apparent indifference and his apparent refusal. Jesus lent her the force of this faith and by lending it made an example of her. Let us therefore pray as this woman did, let us ask for what we believe we should ask for, for ourselves and for others, for souls and for bodies, all for the sake of God's glory. Let us ask for it with absolute faith in the power and goodness of God, so that we will be deeply convinced that our wish will be granted in the end. But God, by virtue of his mercy and goodness, could make us wait some time in order to further sanctify us, through trial, through prayer, through union with him, increased and produced by this ardent, incessant prayer we utter at his feet, unceasingly turned toward the heavens, by extending this act of faith which makes us ask him with complete confidence to answer our prayers, by a thousand other virtuous acts which could emerge from his delay in granting our prayers. Let us note however that when we firmly believe our wishes have been granted, we should not necessarily believe that we will receive what we asked for, but we shall certainly receive either what we asked for or something better. Our Lord, in his infinite goodness, not only wants to answer our prayers but also to rectify our wishes if they are wrongly directed. He promises to grant them and in this way he shares his supreme power with us, but he retains the power to grant us what we ask for or something better. How infinitely and divinely good he is! With what faith we must pray! And how we must pray, how we must ask for ourselves and for others since our prayers are so powerful that they are, through his will, all powerful. Any prayer said with faith produces immense results! Let us pray!

37. "I am. And you will see the Son of Man seated at the right hand of the Power..." (Mk 14:62).

Jesus gave his life for confession of *faith*; it was the immediate cause of his death. With what force, what courage and what love we should confess! Our Lord is therefore a *martyr* in the true sense of the word, a martyr for the confession of the *soul*. The Jews, according to Saint John, pursued him particularly because he called himself the Son of God. In front of Pilate they said he deserved death because he called himself the Son of God. Let us be eager to confess the *faith*, the *faith* in the Son of God, because that is the core of our holy religion, that is what distinguishes it absolutely in one word from so many other false ones. However, in this confession, let us obey, and not do it when we should not. Let us consider that Jesus did not always do it, nor at all times. He kept silent during his hidden life. Even during his public life, he did not always call himself the Son of God. But he did it under certain circumstances. When interrogated by his judges, he always did it. Let us always confess, Jesus Son of God, when interrogated by the judges. Let us always be ready and willing to confess, but although Jesus told us to shout it from the rooftops and to preach the Gospel to all creatures, we should consider that this does not apply equally and in the same way to all Christians, nor to all times and places. We should follow the general or specific rules laid down by the

Holy Church, Christ's spouse. We should obey Jesus in this as in everything, by conforming to the instructions of the Church and those of a wise director. But let us never deny it, that is never allowed; and let us confess it always through our work and our lives. We should not shout our dogma from the rooftops, when our director forbids it, when the Church forbids it, but we should always shout from rooftops Jesus's doctrine, the evangelical spirit, through our lives. And let us fervently wish with all our hearts to be able to also shout out our dogma, our *faith in Jesus*, Son of God, and like our spouse, to give our lives for this, to imitate him, to suffer for the one we love because he said: "No one can have greater love than to lay down his life for his friends" (Jn 15:13).

38. "He reproached them for their incredulity and obstinacy, because they had refused to believe those who had seen him after he had risen" (Mk 16:14).

It is a duty to believe when we have sufficient grounds for credibility to make something morally certain, to exclude all cautious doubt. The reports of trustworthy witnesses who say they have seen something constitute sufficient grounds for credibility and in this case there is a duty to believe. Here the apostles lacked *faith* in two ways—in witnesses who were trustworthy and in God's omnipotence. Moreover, they forgot what Jesus so often predicted—that he would rise from the dead. They lacked the faith they should have had as witnesses worthy of inspiration and whose testimony should have sufficed to make them certain of his resurrection. They also lacked faith because they believed the facts to be impossible; that is, because they believed neither in God's omnipotence nor in Jesus' divinity, or at least their faith was very weak, imperfect and very dormant in them. *Let us believe everything is possible with God, except for things implying contradiction.* When *trustworthy* witnesses maintain they have seen something, *let us believe them*, and especially when they say it is on behalf of God, because then our incredulity, by attacking God's messengers, would attack God himself who sends them.

This is what further increases the error of the apostles. So let us not fall into it!

39. "Whoever believes and is baptized will be saved; whoever does not believe will be condemned" (Mk 16:16).

Such is the value of faith: we cannot be saved without believing. It is not absolutely necessary to be baptized by water, although baptism is a necessary means. It is a necessary means but not an absolute one, because we can be baptized by desire. However, we must believe not in all dogma, but in certain ones. Above all we must believe in God, we must believe in God punishing the wicked and rewarding the chosen. Such faith is necessary for salvation because everyone can and *must* attain it only by the light of natural reason helped by inner grace of which God provides enough for everyone. *We must at least believe in this, in God the retributor, and have the willingness to do absolutely everything he wants of us and to believe absolutely everything he wants us to believe. With these feelings we are in the Church of desire.*

But to go to heaven, must we believe specifically in something more, or are our desires and our good will not enough? Theologians debate this topic and some say that there are two dogmas, the dogma of Incarnation and the dogma of the Holy Trinity, which must be believed in specifically for salvation, when the Gospel has been preached. They call these dogmas "truths of means," the way baptism is a "means." However, it appears that—like baptism—they are not absolute means, but faith in God the Retributor, together with the strong and true will to do and believe everything he wants us to actually entering the Church, by desire, suffices for specific faith. Otherwise this would make the "baptism of desire" often useless, since it would limit the possibility of salvation to Christians only. That means that there would be no possible salvation for Moslems once the Gospel was preached to them, and this is not what the Church believes. It teaches that faith in God the Retributor and the will to obey all his commandments and to please him in everything is enough to be in the

Church "by desire—as it is to be baptized by desire"—and consequently to be saved, if one has no mortal sin on one's conscience at the time of death, either through preserved innocence or through perfect penitence. Of course, such faith and good will depend on the lack of specific faith in other truths and stem not from negligence or lack of faithfulness but from invincible ignorance. Such innocence, such perfect penitence and good will are difficult to achieve for those not having true religion. Good is difficult to achieve for those of us who have the truth to guide us, the sacraments, the examples of Our Lord, our religious directors as support, we over whom the devil, because of baptism, sacraments, rituals and grace, has lost so much of his power. What infinite difficulties surround those who are in such darkness and deprived of so much good! We must therefore also wish and ask for faith for them, just as we must pray for them and do everything in our power to have God make them finally open their eyes to the truths of the Gospel! We should work toward this goal and do all we can for these lost ones whom Our Lord wants to save, for these sheep whom he said must be led, so there will be but one fold and one shepherd for these souls for whom he gave all his blood! Concerning the issue of whether it is enough for salvation to have faith in God the Retributor, to show the good will to do and believe everything he asks of us, and to demonstrate invincible ignorance of other truths of means, I am not absolutely certain I have precisely expressed the belief of the Church, to which I subject myself entirely. I retract absolutely everything which does not conform with the Church in what I have just written, and in everything I have ever said or written. And I hereby declare that I want always to be entirely subjected to the Church in thought, words and deeds. Amen.

What consequences these grave words of Our Lord have for me: without seeking to enter the darkness, I let myself be led there *mistakenly*, since because of my ignorance I am incapable of safely meditating on such words without a guide, but because of the grace of God they are fruitful, since they have made my ignorance clear to me. Without going into detail, I must draw two conclusions from these words: my *gratefulness* that God not only gave me baptism, faith, a pious education and such good religious instruction, but furthermore restored my faith in his mercy, after I had lost it through my own fault and was so unconcerned about recovering it; the *spiritual zeal* for all those who have no faith. What pain for Jesus' heart! What pain for mine if I am united in spirit to my Spouse. What zeal, what desires, if I had his spirit. My Jesus, My Lord, my God, my beloved, give me your spirit, the good spirit you cannot refuse, give me that spiritual zeal, the charity which you so want me to have! Amen. Oh, how much there is to humiliate me and for me to ask for when I see the zeal I should have and my coldness. Sacred Heart of Jesus, forgive me, help me, rescue me!

I just found in a notebook what the theologians teach concerning the faith needed to be saved. Faith is necessary for justification, not only necessarily as a *precept* but also necessarily as a *means*. The justifying faith must extend *virtually and specifically* to the entire purpose of the Catholic faith and *presently and explicitly*, at least to the truths of God's existence and his rewarding and punishing. Is faith in the mysteries of the Trinity and the Incarnation necessarily a means? That is debatable. In practice, it is preferable to believe in them. Sinners may obtain the mercy of justification through the rites of baptism or those of penitence, or without any rites, simply through the desire for them. The will to do God's will in everything contains the implicit desire of these rites, for those who are unaware of them.

LUKE

40. "Having seen their faith, he said: My friend, your sins are forgiven you" (Lk 5:20).

It is in response to the *faith* of these people that our Lord cured not the body of their friend, which they were asking for, but something infinitely greater—his soul—although they did not think of asking for it. It often happens this way: we ask for one thing and we neglect to ask for another which is a thousand times more desirable. But however rash our wish may be, God takes pity on us and if we have prayed with *faith*, *faith* in his goodness and power, *faith* that in his incomparable goodness and his promises, he will certainly grant us what we ask for or something better, then God in his mercy answers our prayers and grants us either what we asked for or what we would have asked for if we had been wiser, what we should have asked for, what is most desirable for us, as he did here.

Let us therefore pray for ourselves and for others. These people prayed for their neighbors; Jaire and the Canaanite prayed for their neighbors and we can see how their prayers were answered. Let us pray for our neighbors with great *faith* and we shall receive; we shall receive what we asked for or something better. Let us ask for goodness in the spirit of others and ourselves: Jesus said he would never refuse it. Let us ask for everything which we believe would benefit souls and bodies, seeing Jesus in all persons, and asking for everyone what we would ask for Jesus: goodness primarily for the soul and then for the body. Let us pray for this with *faith* and our prayers will never be in vain. God's goodness could not be anything less than the idea we have of it. His promise is absolute, any prayers said with faith will always be answered. We will always receive either what we have asked for or something better. Often the better thing is well hidden, and is not obvious, but we will certainly receive it. Here is an example: Catherine of Genoa often prayed for a person to be delivered from certain faults and upon her surprise that her prayers were not answered by Jesus, he appeared before her and said: "If I deliver this person from these faults, which are insignificant and keep him humble, he will spend three years in purgatory. If I let them be, he will go straight to heaven."

41. "...He went to the mountain to pray; and he spent the whole night in prayer to God" (Lk 6:12).

If we had enough faith in these words, with what ardor we would endeavor to spend entire nights in prayer, as did so many saints, faithfully imitating Jesus, such as Saint Francis of Assisi, Saint Anthony the Great, and so many others! What a gap between this example of our Lord and my half-heartedness, my cowardice! But he gave this example so that it would be followed, since he so blessed those of his saints who followed him. Oh my God, give me this *faith*, this love, this courage...this *faith* which makes one follow you with confidence, zealously stepping into your footsteps. Amen.

42. "Give and there will be gifts for you...because the standard you use will be the standard used for you" (Lk 6:38).

Oh my God, if we had faith in these words, how different our lives would be! How different our thoughts, words and actions would be. How much more gentle, tender, kindly, compassionate and loving our thoughts would be! How much more affectionate, encouraging and pure our actions would be, leading us to God! How unselfish, charitable and edifying our actions would be! How we would do for our neighbors, whoever they were, absolutely everything they needed from us in the interest of their bodies and souls, truly seeing Jesus in them! And it is Jesus who receives everything we do for others for the sake of him. We must believe this with *faith* (cf. Mt 25). My God, give me *faith*, the faith which transforms life, may it transform mine; may I live from it, since "the upright will live through faith" (Gal 3:11). Amen.

43. "Not even in Israel have I found faith as great as this" (Lk 7:9).

Jesus thus commended the *faith* of the centurion. This faith is, above all, absolute faith in his power, in the power which makes everything so easy for him. "Let my boy be cured by giving your word" (Lk 7:7), said the centurion. Saint Bernard said the same to his brother, frightened upon seeing him perform his first miracles. "If you only knew how easy it is for God!" The righteous live on faith—they see God's action in everything, be it slightly hidden or more apparent. Regardless of whether God's wonders are obvious or whether divine power is revealed in ordinary or extraordinary effects, little can astonish faith! Everything is so easy for God! God is so powerful and so good! How could he astonish us? Only one thing is impossible for him and that is to not be perfect, to not be good, to not live up to his word. He promised to answer prayers said with faith. Let us pray, let us pray constantly for ourselves whom God loves, for all people, whom he loves so much that he gave his blood for them, that he loves so much that we can do nothing to please him more than to pray for them through love for him, and be sure that if asked with faith, our prayers will always, always be answered, in accordance with his promise. When they do not seem to be answered, they are actually answered even better, since that means that God has instead given us something better still.

44. "Your faith has saved you; go in peace," Jesus said to Saint Magdalene (Lk 7:50).

At the end he attributed this salvation *to faith*, which he also attributed to love. In order to love, we must have faith. To love we must know, and while we are here on earth, where we cannot see, where we know God only by faith, the measure of love is that of faith. We love to the extent that we believe. My God, give us faith, intense faith, ardent faith, forever focusing on you, on your words, and which is the root of the greatest love. "The upright will live through faith" and love.

Give us faith, my God, the greatest faith and the greatest love. Faith breeds love, but love then infinitely increases faith. They strengthen one another, they constantly reinforce each other, because the more faith we have, the more we love, and the more we love, the more we value the faith in the beloved. My God, make these two virtues in me continuously develop and stimulate each other, and not stop growing until my faith becomes clear sight, through your great mercy. Amen.

45. *"Your faith has saved you; go in peace," Jesus said to the hemorrhaging woman (Lk 8:48).*

She believed in Jesus' power and goodness and believed that she could be cured of her ailments just by touching him. And Jesus was pleased to cure her to reward her for this faith, because that faith honored him. Thus, throughout the centuries he rewarded those with such intense faith through miracles: Saint Bernard and many others.

In his supreme goodness, he does not want to show less goodness than that attributed to him. He intends to show that his mercy rests above all our desires, our thoughts, everything that we can imagine. However, even when he enjoys answering all our prayers concretely and immediately, he reserves the right to rectify our wishes and grant us not what we ask for but something better. Examples can be found in the history of great miracle workers. Saint Martin and Saint Bernard did not always have their prayers answered in the way they wanted; they received more. Saint Bernard asked for the physical life of his brother, for him to be cured on earth. And God granted Gerald eternal life, the cure for all pain and immediate entry to heaven.[7]

Let us pray a lot, let us pray and pray. The more we ask for, with absolute faith, the more we shall receive. Our prayers can never equal God's power or goodness, but the greater they are, the more numerous they are, and said with faith, the more

---

[7] *Saint Bernard,* Sermons super Cantica, *(Ed. J. Leclercq, Rome, 1957). Serm. 26, Vol. I, p. 169-181.*

they will honor him because they will more clearly reflect how great we believe his goodness and his power are, and consequently he will encourage them by answering them concretely and immediately. Let us thus ask with absolute faith that our prayers be granted, that we receive what we have asked for or better, and let us therefore ask for as much as possible, the greatest benefits for others and for ourselves constantly. The more we ask for, if we do so with faith, the more we honor God. And as our prayers are always answered, we shall thus accomplish a twofold precept: We shall glorify God and do the greatest good to others.

46. "Do not be afraid, only have faith" (Lk 8:50).

What our Lord told Jaire, he told all of us. Let us not fear. What have we to fear? Let us only believe. Let us believe deep within our souls these divine words, which are so comforting, so certain: "Those who have been called in accordance with his purpose, and [God] turns everything to their good.... Not one sparrow falls to the ground without your Father knowing.... You are worth much more than sparrows.... Every hair on your head has been counted.... Seek first the kingdom of God and his righteousness and these other things will be given you besides.... I am capable of everything with the one who strengthens me...."

Let us believe that God is Almighty and that nothing, not the slightest thing, will happen without his permission and that he loves us infinitely. Let us believe, let us fear neither people, nor things, nor demons, but let us be aware that nothing can harm us and that everything happens for our greatest benefit, if we are faithful to grace. Let us believe, let us not fear being unable to fulfill God's commands to us. He is Almighty and we are capable of everything with the one who strengthens us. Let us not fear. He loves us infinitely and he is Almighty. Let us only believe this and have but one concern: to be faithful to his grace and do everything to carry out his will.

47. "The least among you all is the one who is the greatest" (Lk 9:48).

"...For everyone who raises himself up will be humbled, but anyone who humbles himself will be raised up" (cf. Lk 18:14). "For what is highly esteemed in human eyes is loathsome in the sight of God" (Lk 16:15). If we relate to these words, if we receive them with *faith*, how we would cherish everything which lowers us—humility, obedience, simplicity, abjection, humiliation! How we would seek the bottom rung, obscurity, abjection, humiliation, poverty! How we would bury ourselves! "The life you have is hidden with Christ in God" (cf. Col 3:3). How we would descend! How we would make ourselves small and humble! How we would try to be unknown and appear ignorant! How we would try to hide any God-given gifts! How we would flee any external elevation! And if by duty we were forced to accept any, how we would preserve our humility, show ourselves to be simple, friends of the small, humble friends of the abject and poor! And if we could always remain in deep abjection, how we would plunge into it with joy and try to be "a worm and not a man" (Ps 21:7), to make ourselves the last of the last, small, poor, scorned, ignorant, demented, unknown in the eyes of everybody and deeply humble in our own. For, alas, each moment of each day is for us to humiliate ourselves. Oh my God, who has given me this infinite blessing to somewhat understand these truths, deign to increase my *faith* and make me enter into abjection, humility, obscurity and humiliation. Put me at the bottom in the eyes of everyone including myself, more and more everyday. Deign to make me the smallest of all, in everyone's eyes including my own, in you, through you and for you, my beloved Master. Amen!

48. "The lamp of your body is your eye. When your eye is clear, your whole body, too, is filled with light; but when it is diseased your body, too, will be darkened" (Lk 11:34).

What is this lamp of our soul which depends on us for brightness or darkness? The Fathers are divided and have various interpretations. Some say: "Our light is purpose. If it is pure, all our actions are good; if it is bad, all our actions are bad." Others say: "It is intelligence. If it is not darkened by passions, it brightens the soul, we are in the light. If passions dominate it, it is blinded, it no longer distinguishes the truth and the entire soul has no guide and is in darkness." Many say: "This is faith. Faith enlightens reason. May faith enlighten our souls and guide our understanding. We are in the light, we walk in the brightness of the sun of truth. Should faith become shrouded, as among the indifferent, should it become spoiled as among heretics, should it disappear as among the incredulous, then our sun has disappeared, reason no longer has its beacon, no longer has the rule which prevented it from deviating, no longer has the luminous column showing it the way, the soul is in darkness. The upright live through faith; they walk in its light and are enlightened by it in all their acts. It is a torch which they carry everywhere, and if they happen to miss it, they lose all their light, they are in darkness, they cannot act, there is nothing to guide them, they grope in the dark, they cannot act, they are in the darkest night." My God, always give me an absolutely straight purpose! Give me understanding free of all passions! Give me faith, perfectly pure faith which illuminates all my steps, guides all my acts, and directs all my thoughts, words and actions. Amen!

49. "Now if that is how God clothes a flower which is growing wild today and is thrown into the furnace tomorrow, how much more will he look after you, who have so little faith!" (Lk 12:28).

Here Jesus chastises us for our lack of faith, all of us who worry about food and clothing instead of knowing that everything comes from God alone. Both the wealth of the rich and the bread of the poor are given by him, the fruit of the earth, the products of industry and profits from trade only appear to be the result of our labor. We work, and God causes growth, germination and ripening. God causes prosperity. God does everything. Everything comes from him, from his power, which supports everything, brings everything into being. God is the only one to make things happen, he is necessary for the slightest act, the slightest existence; everything can be found in his immensity.

Let us not worry, because we can do nothing on our own. Let us turn toward the only one who can give us what we need, and let us expect it of him without anxiety, for two reasons: God's goodness and our own ignorance. His *goodness* because, as he tells us here, he will definitely give us what we need since he is so good and gives so liberally to the merest of creatures. How could he not provide what is necessary, considering the way he gives food to the birds and clothes to the flowers, to people, who were redeemed at the cost of his Son's blood?

Our ignorance is such that we practically never know whether or not it is better for our soul to have a given spiritual or temporal good. We can — and in fact *must* — repeatedly ask for spiritual goods for ourselves and our neighbors, but preferably for the goods that God urgently wants us to have: the glorification of his Name, his reign in all souls, the accomplishment of his will, etc.

Actually, we can pray for anything, both material and spiritual goods, either for ourselves or for our neighbors, when it seems appropriate for God's glory, but when it is something other than a blessing obviously desired by God, we must always add "yet not as I will, but as you will" (Mt 26:39). And our prayers regarding material things should be very brief, just a few words, because first of all we are profoundly unaware of whether it is good for us to have them, however necessary they may seem; and secondly, because God forbids us here to worry about them and promises us to always provide them in so far as they are good, since he gives them to inanimate objects.

But above all, we must never expect anything from people or from ourselves. We must not worry, because everything is in God's hands and he will always give us what is truly good for us, since not a hair can fall off our heads without his permission and he takes care of all of his creatures, giving them everything necessary for daily life, after having given them existence. My God, give me *faith*, ban from my soul any concern for daily bread, material existence. Leave only absolute trust in you, trust in your Providence; leave only one desire, that your will be done; only one request, that your heart be comforted, that you be glorified, that your holy will be accomplished. Amen.

Our Lord doesn't mean here that we must not ask for anything—he so often tells us to ask. But he means we should ask without worry, with absolute trust and *faith*: If requests are useful for you, they have already been granted before being expressed, and since when they have to do with material goods, you never know whether or not you should want something. But what you do know, what I am telling you, is that I will give you what is good for you if you ask for it. I will even give it to you if you don't ask for it.

You should thus not be at all concerned. Have *faith* that you will always have the basics, what is really useful. When it seems to be missing, that is because it isn't *truly useful* to you; that means that it is better for you to endure such deprivation. Therefore, never say to yourself: How will I eat tomorrow? That should never concern you: *I alone* feed you today and it will be as easy for me to do so tomorrow as it is for me to do so today.

Have *faith* in my goodness, in my Word, in your ignorance. *Believe* that everything comes from *me alone*, that neither you nor anyone else could obtain a single piece of bread without me, and that I can do everything without anyone. So never let any concern for material things enter your soul: I am here, I see you, I am good, I am almighty, I love you and I promised never to let you need anything. Is that not enough for you? Why would you seek help from people, referring to their liberality, your own prudence or your own industry? Why should you worry? See what an insult to me that would be! What an insult, what folly, and what ultimate impiety!

However, while requests and prayers spurred by worry are ungratefulness and impiety, requests made with *faith*, with perfect, wholehearted *faith*, are pleasing to God. They testify to love: we love to make requests on our beloved. They are a sign of trust in God, recognizing that we expect everything from him alone; they don't mean telling him not to forget us, they mean saying to him: You told us a hundred times in the Gospel: "Ask!" I am obeying you, my God, I am asking for something, this is what I need. I firmly believe that you will give me what is best for me because you are good and all-powerful and you promised me you would. Praying with faith means telling God: I want to obey you in everything, my God, and you said to me: "Ask!" I am therefore asking you for this, even though I know that you can see what I need and that you, who are so good, wouldn't let me lack anything that is truly useful to me. I am asking you out of obedience.

God has plenty of reasons to command us to make requests. It forces us to raise our eyes toward him, to think about him. It keeps us from forgetting him and institutes a constant dialogue between our souls and him. That is why God so often makes us feel spiritual or material needs. When used for what God gave them to us for, these often painful needs and deprivations provide our souls with the greatest relief, that of prayer, constant prayer, a sigh, a constant focus of the soul on God. God uses this means to unite with our souls if they are faithful to this grace through constant prayer. What infinite good he provides through such needs! How good he is! How admirable his ways!

50. "Seek out instead his kingship over you, and the rest will follow in turn" (Lk 12:31).

My God, please give me faith in these words and let them guide my life: to seek you, to do your will, never to worry at all about the rest, assuming that after that, whatever happens to us will be a gift from your hand and, whether it looks good or bad that you will give us something good for our souls, a favor, a blessing from you, something specifically designed for our sanctification.

Your will is for us to be holy, perfect, doing everything that seems most saintly, most perfect, what we think you would have done in our place. Let us not be concerned by the rest, but let us be convinced that you will give us everything we need, be they spiritual or material needs. When we suffer from drought or want, darkness or disease, inner pain or outer persecution, anguish of the soul or agony of the body, let us still bless our Father and the heart of our Spouse. What he gives us is what is most appropriate for our souls; it is a blessing, a grace, a means of sanctification.

As long as I am faithful I am sure to have an abundance of all goods. If I seek them purely, I am sure that it is good for me. "The heavens and the earth will pass away but my word will not pass" (Mt 24:35). Let us therefore never wonder: How will I live tomorrow? Where will I be? Let us only wonder what it would be most perfect to do at the present time, let us do it and let us firmly *believe* that if we seek the kingdom of God and his righteousness, the rest will follow in turn.

51. "Do not live in fear, little flock. It has pleased your Father to give you the kingdom" (Lk 12:32).

If we have *faith* in that word, how many fears we would feel far from us, except the fear of displeasing the King our Spouse. How we would live in joy and gratitude, feeling the greatness of our duties, thinking about the higher saintliness our Father is calling us to, the perfection! He gives us the kingdom of heaven to hope for. Through Holy Communion he makes us Christ's spouses crowned with his diadem. What a joy! What recognition!

But such happiness entails great duties. How saintly the Holy Church's children must be! God wants them to be spotless, without a wrinkle, immaculate. Those children were so showered with goods by their mother, so well cared for, so strengthened, and have received so much from her, everything they need to be perfect. She has given them, in such abundance and with such wisdom, the guidance of a knowledgeable spiritual director, the nourishment of the Holy Books, the saints, joint prayer, the Commandments and advice, everything, absolutely everything, and above all the Blessed Sacrament. How holy must those called to the kingdom of heaven be to live with God, to possess God for eternity. Nothing soiled will enter into heavenly Jerusalem. How holy Jesus' spouse must be, being married to a living King, forever under his gaze, pleasing or displeasing him through all our acts, all our thoughts, our words and our actions, at every moment of our lives, able to comfort his heart by doing what is most perfect at every moment of our lives.

Oh, my Lord Jesus, my Spouse, you who make me Queen, I beg of you, since through your almighty grace my life is now changing and you are showing me so clearly right now how much so, as your spouse crowned with your crown, I must comfort you by doing what is most perfect at every moment, let me do so, let me correct myself, let me no longer slip back into the faults I so often, so miserably succumb to!

This moment means my life is being corrected! There are three faults in particular for which I beg you for forgiveness on my knees, my Lord, and from which I beseech you to deliver me, as well as all the others: halfheartedness in prayer, my failure to keep the thought of your presence in mind and my laziness in getting up in the morning.

Forgive me, forgive me, for those faults and the others! Oh, my Spouse, my Master! You who love me, please forgive me for these faults, correct them for me and let me comfort you in the future by always doing what is most perfect, in you, through you and for you. Amen.

52. *"Sell whatever you have and give alms. Get purses for yourselves that do not wear out, a never-failing treasure with the Lord" (Lk 12:33).*

My God, let us receive these words with *faith*! With what detachment, poverty, charity and alms we would live if we firmly *believed* these words. Yes, the best way to use our money, the most perfect way to spend it, the most economical investment for it is not to purchase a house, clothing or food for a day but to find a home in the heavens and clothe ourselves in glory in Paradise, that is, to invest our money not to produce interest for a few years of our life but for the infinity of eternity.

What good will our wealth on earth do us, be it big or small, or our savings, our well-being, our fortune on earth, be it big or small, in a few years, or perhaps in a few days? While what we will have given to the poor will earn us more of the unutterable happiness of heaven, less of the terrible pains of purgatory and perhaps deliverance from hell! Oh, my God! Give us faith in this word and teach us to sell what we have to give it in alms and to buy at that price the infinite joy of seeing you and loving you in heaven as much as you want us to, in you, through you and for you.

53. "More will be asked of a man to whom more has been entrusted" (Lk 12:48).

My God, how this word was meant for me and how I need to receive it with *faith*, since I have received so much! Oh, how I wish I had *faith* in that word, the faith I should have, practical faith, profound faith inspiring my thoughts, my words and my works, life-altering faith, the faith the righteous live by. I beg of you to give me that faith, my beloved Jesus, you who allow me to be at your feet right now, who called me here and who unfortunately called me here before but in vain. (Forgive me! Forgive me! Forgive me!)

That faith would give me the fear of God that is the beginning of wisdom. I would see the immensity of my duties, since I have received so much. I would see how high I must climb, since I have been so blessed for that purpose. How brave and generous I would be, knowing that having received so much, I've been blessed to do so and that I must give a very great deal, since I have received so, so much.

How fervent I would be! How rapidly I would correct the three vices I suffer from almost every day: halfheartedness in prayer, neglect in keeping the presence of God in mind and laziness in getting up in the morning. How humble I would be, seeing the immensity of what I must give and the little that I do give.

Oh, my God, in you, through you and for you, give me that *faith*, give me a sense of the *grandness of my duties*, so that I may finally begin to carry them out, so that I may be what you want me to, so that I may comfort your heart, in you, through you and for you. Amen!

54. "There will be more joy in heaven over one repentant sinner than over 99 righteous people who have no need to repent" (Lk 15:7).

My God, if we really had *faith* in this word, how zealously we would pray, how penitent we would be, how we would do everything possible to get sinners to convert! That would be the essence of our prayers, our work, our lives, the essence, not for its own sake but for the sake of you who are the only essence, my Lord and my God! That would be secondary in our hearts, but would require the most time and work. And it would only be in imitation of you.

You came to seek out and save those who were lost (cf. Mt 18:11). What else were the three years of public life you had used for if not to seek out and save the lost sheep? And who could say with what love you prayed and what desires you expressed to your Father for that purpose during your hidden life? Teach me to do so too, my God.

Teach me to want, to ask for and to seek the conversion of sinners with the passion appropriate for the love of your glory, for the comfort of your heart, for the love of my neighbors. Considering how this twofold love demands that we wish for those souls—the souls of your beloved children, of our brothers and sisters in you—to praise you and love you eternally instead of hating you and profaning your name eternally, it is easy to see that it is right that one repentant sinner should cause more joy than 99 righteous people!

My God, may I be for sinners what I should be, in my thoughts, my words and my actions, in you, through you and for you. Amen!

55. "No servant can have two masters.... You cannot give yourself to God and money" (Lk 16:13).

Oh, my God, if we had faith in these words, how our inner and outer lives would change! We cannot have two masters: we must belong to God alone. We must rid ourselves of everything else in order to be full of God. And we cannot be full of him if we are not devoid of all the rest. There isn't room in our heart for two masters; if our heart is full of one, it cannot share with another. God has the right to fill our entire heart. In order for him to do so it must be devoid of anything else.

Let us empty our heart, empty it, empty it completely, so that Jesus can fill it, reign in it, be its only Master. Let us empty it of ourselves, of our pride. Let us empty it of attachment to other creatures, to certain people. Let us empty it of attachment to material things. Let us empty it of everything that is not God, and then we can begin to love God.

We cannot love at once God and ourselves or God and money. As long as we can feel an attachment to money in ourselves, we cannot love God, our heart isn't empty, it cannot belong entirely to its Creator. In order not to love money, we must not need it, and must therefore live in poverty. If we do not live in poverty, then we need money, want money, love money. Let us empty ourselves of everything to belong entirely to God. Let us eliminate the needs that we can in order to be devoid of any desire, any concern and be dominated only by God, our only Master.

56. "What man thinks important, God holds in contempt" (Lk 16:15).

Our Lord was referring here to wealth, and he was saying this to the Pharisees, so that it must be understood as meaning wealth, the honor wealth confers and human esteem in general. If we receive this word with *faith*, my God, how the lives of many souls would change! Those seeking wealth and honor, either for themselves or for their loved ones or for their order or their house if they are religious, would seek it no longer. And they would steep themselves with love in mediocrity, darkness, poverty and smallness!

Those who have wealth, are honored and who, while not seeking to acquire more wealth and honor than they already have, are very careful to preserve what they do have, either for themselves or for others, out of a sense of duty, would care little about preserving such wealth if they understood with *faith* your Word telling them that they are an abomination to you, if they looked at your examples with faith, you who constantly rejected them!

Those who are poor and held in contempt, far from suffering, worrying and growing bitter, would feel profoundly happy, would be jubilant to the depths of their souls, would thank you endlessly for having so mercifully given them the better share, the one you most prefer, the one that is most pleasing to you. That is the share you chose for yourself for every day of your life. You covered yourself with poverty and contempt like an inseparable cloak. You were born in such poverty and contempt and lived and died in it.

You tried to teach people that "blest are the poor, blest are those persecuted!" (Mt 5:3; 5:10). That is one of the truths you were most intent on inculcating: contempt for worldly goods, human honors, human esteem, any worldly elevation, along with the knowledge that everything the earth can and does produce is nothing, not only nothing, but harmful, (even if not evil in itself) because it harms the soul by removing it from God. Worldly goods are bushes preventing the divine seeds from germinating. They create false values, for as soon as we feel the slightest esteem for them, we have esteem for something other than God, which is where the falsehood lies, since any creature is nothing next to God. All our esteem, all our love, belongs to God alone!

To make us see this truth, the truth of absolute contempt for any wealth, any honor, any earthly good, any human esteem, you have given us countless words and examples. Because of the lesson you have given us your entire life, you not only rejected wealth, but embraced the worst poverty, not only rejected honors but embraced the worst shame, first the darkness of the poorest workers, then the contempt spawned by seducers, impostors and blasphemers, and finally the horror inspired by criminals and convicts sentenced to death.

In your hidden life, you thus lived poorer and were held in greater contempt than the poorest and most disrespected worker, because you wanted to teach us contempt for all wealth and human esteem. You spent your public life with nowhere to lay your head (cf. Mt 8:20), persecuted, driven out of every town, poorer and held in greater contempt than any missionary. And not one day in your life did you stop shouting from the rooftops through your word and your example that we must despise material goods and human esteem.

My Lord Jesus, let us receive these words and examples with *faith* and let us base our lives on them. And as for me, whom you have chosen because of my wretchedness in order to fill me with your favors, since you like to give to the poor, me whom you have a thousand and one times blessed allowing me to be a faithful image of your hidden life and to shout your Gospel from the rooftops, not through my words but through my life, let me imitate you, oh, my God, and shout out your Gospel by practicing your example, the poverty and abjection of the poorest worker held in the greatest contempt, as you want me to, in you, through you and for you. Amen. Thank you, thank you, thank you, my God!

57. "If you had faith the size of a mustard seed, you could say to this sycamore, 'Be uprooted and transplanted into the sea,' and it would obey you" (Lk 17:6).

This can be interpreted literally, as in Saint Gregory Thaumaturge and the mountain, the staffs of several saints which suddenly turned into tall trees or the floods and fires miraculously stopped. It can also be interpreted figuratively, as in the instant conversions, the virtues arising so unexpectedly in souls flooded with passion.

That is the force of prayer, believing prayer, having steadfast *faith* that it will be answered because the asker believes in three things: the infinite *goodness* and infinite *power* of God and the *veracity* of his words, words in which he often promised in the Holy Gospel always to respond to our faith. People's prayers will be answered if they have unwavering *faith* that if they pray with humility and trust they will receive, either what they are seeking for or something better than what they are asking for, and that in any event, their prayers, far from being useless and ignored, will always, always be useful, will always, always be answered and will always obtain good, either what they are asking for or (God's goodness being so great) something better. God is so good that he sets no limits on the effectiveness of our prayers, but since no matter how great our requests are his power and goodness will always surpass them, he allows himself to give us even more than we ask for. My God, give me that *faith*, and since my prayers can do so much good, may I pray and pray and pray, for myself, for those you have placed beside me in my life. Let me pray to you with profound *faith* in the effectiveness of humble, believing prayers *the way* you want me to pray, with that humility and faith, and let me pray to you *as much as* you want me to, for your glory, for the good of your children, to do the most good for your children and thus to glorify you the most, in you, through you and for you. Amen!

58. "He told them a parable on the necessity of praying always and not losing heart" (Lk 18:1).

This refers to the parable Jesus told about the corrupt judge. If we had *faith* in this parable, in these words of Jesus, how we would incessantly pray, how we would dispel temptations with prayer, if not quickly (because they could return), at least bravely and without letting ourselves be overcome. How we would obtain blessings for others and ourselves, how our lives would be always directed toward heaven, in a continuous request. We have so much to ask for, if we love our neighbors, if we feel our misery, that is, if we have a shadow of charity and humility. My God, give me this *faith*, the faith in your words which gives us faith in our prayers. Make our lives, which we only want to be what you want them to be, lives which like your own, make blessings shower down on all people at every moment, through prayer in you, for you and through you. Amen!

59. "There is one thing further you must do. Sell all you have and give it to the poor. You will have treasure in heaven. Then come and follow me" (Lk 18:22).

My God, make me embrace these words with *faith*. It seems so simple yet it is so difficult, and who acts on it? It must be something perfect since only saints do it. Aside from saints, who considers alms to the poor an investment in heaven? Who, except them, give with the eagerness inspired by such faith? Oh, how human life would change, how points of view would change, how different deeds would be if this *faith* entered souls. To give alms to the poor surely places one in heaven, changing a transitory and perishable asset into an eternal one! If only we actually believed this! Alas, how far we are from this, even those of us who think of ourselves as religious souls!

Who follows Jesus by taking the same path as he, imitating him in everything, truly seeing him as the path, "following" him as the apostles followed him in the union of souls which "followed" his own, forming and modeling themselves perfectly after his soul, in the union of their external life, going where he wanted to go, sharing his poverty, his abjection, everything he wanted to suffer, being what he wanted to be, "following" him by sharing and imitating everything in his interior and exterior life. Who does this, except the saints? Oh, my God, spread *faith* in your words on earth, give it to me, to those whom I must love even more, give it to all your children. Teach me to have faith in charity by considering it a treasure inscribed in heaven and to follow you by imitating you in everything, by imitating your faithful images.

60. "How hard it will be for the rich to go into the kingdom of God" (Lk 18:24).

Oh my Lord Jesus, if we really had *faith* in these words, how we would dread wealth and fortune! And how we would rejoice in poverty, destitution and view such hardships as blessings! Yes, if lack of money is a blessing, the difficulties and material and moral hardships that it produces are also blessings: You glorify yourself and sanctify us through them. They mean resembling you, my beloved Savior, you who all your life ate the bread of the poor and so rarely avoided suffering: You have no doubt tasted that bitterness.

Let us therefore not say: Give us generously what we need. God promised the basics, he will give us what we need. God promised us the basics, he did not promise us the means to lead a comfortable life, let alone a life of luxury and prosperity, he who was always in hardship. The basics are strictly what the poor need to live, what the poor people of the country live on. The basics are sometimes even less, because there may be moments in life when we can get by, without any danger to the spirit or body, despite major deprivations. There are hardly any poor people who do not sometimes have times like this. Let us avoid all *comfort* in life. A comfortable life, in the guise of spiritual comfort, deceives us and leads us very far from Nazareth, very far from the poor home, from the poor manger of the Holy Family. A comfortable life means comfort of the human, worldly spirit. Jesus was poor, so poor that he could not lead it. Having no means to buy his daily food, he had to ration the basics and give alms.

If the love of God and imitation of Jesus restricts, rejects and denies comfort in life, which people praise and view as desirable and compatible with poverty, love for one's neighbors also rejects it. Love of our neighbors makes us severely restrict any personal spending in order to give as much as possible to the poor. Saint Thomas of Villanova shocked a tailor by wearing the same vest for more than twelve years, but he then gave him a large sum of money for the dowry of his daughters and the tailor's shock was replaced by admiration. This is not being mean-spirited but rather depriving oneself as much as possible in order to give as much as possible to others, to Jesus in the guise of the poor. On the contrary, it is being truly generous.

But if we cannot either give to others or have enough for ourselves, if we cannot do whatever seems good, useful and necessary due to lack of money, *let us further rejoice: such destitution, such want, such a lack of the basics are similarities with Jesus, and resemblance to our beloved is the utmost in sweetness and blessings*. But my God, since it is so good not to have money, to lack everything, would it be better not to work at all for a living and never seek to have money? No, "he who does not work, does not eat" (1 Th 3:10), I said through the mouth of Saint Paul. And I gave the example of workers who work for a living and receive my salary. I gave the example of the life of the apostles, who received what they needed to live from holy women. We must try to have money to the extent that it is *right*, and through the *most righteous* means.

The means are known to everyone according to their situation, differing for a missionary or a worker. The extent of the means depends on personal circumstances: it varies for a worker, a monk, a bishop or a king. The quantity necessary to give to everyone, to God, to oneself, to one's neighbor, is that which is *right* to give them. For workers, it is very little: daily bread for themselves, a small amount of alms for the poor and leisure time to pray to God. Even for simple workers, *in exceptional cases,* there can be more, if the workers have debts, and they can have legitimate, honorable debts, debts inherited from parents or incurred during a long illness or while caring for sick relatives, or to help a friend. In the case of debts, there is *obligation of justice* to try to have the money by the just means available in order to pay back what one owes.

Thank you, God, for having explained everything to me so clearly. Now, let us go back to the beginning and give me what I beg of you, to give me and those whom you want me to love in particular, to all your children, this dread of money and this love of poverty, this tender and joyous acceptance of poverty, of neediness, of all the sufferings which they entail. Give us dread, contempt for money and the comfortable life it affords, give us a love for poverty and the austere life to which it leads us. Let us embrace these characteristics of Jesus! My God, give us faith in your words, give us your spirit, in you, through you and for you. Amen!

61. "Receive your sight, your faith has healed you" (Lk 18:42).

Jesus attributed the blind man's cure to his faith. His prayers were answered because he prayed with *faith*, faith in the power and goodness of God. These two motives suffice to force us to pray with *faith*, to make it a *duty* for us. We know that God is infinitely powerful and good: that is enough that we *should believe* that our prayers will always be granted, unless our prayers themselves are an offense against God, if they asked for success in evil deeds or if they were arrogant, irreverent, etc.

But there is a third reason for faith which not only eliminates any motives but also any excuse for not having faith that our prayers will always be answered. This third motive is the word of Our Lord who tells us and repeats a hundred times that prayers said with faith will always be *answered* (that is, that he will always grant whatever we ask for or something better). Oh Lord Jesus, you who told me to love you above all, to love all people as you have loved them, how I must be a man of desires if I have these two loves in my heart, how I must desire your glorification and sanctification of people! How I must pray for them! My God, teach me to pray for them, make my life a life of prayer, make me pray incessantly, as you have incessantly prayed, in you, through you and for you!

62. *"If anyone should ask you: 'why are you untying the beast,' say, 'the maker has need of it' "* (Lk 19:31).

Sometimes you ask us, my God, for things which we do not understand, as you did here with the apostles. In those cases we must have faith. We must obey with faith, blindly, without understanding. Our directors and religious superiors could force us to do things which although not seeming bad to us, do seem useless, inappropriate, less than perfect or that they might stop us from doing things which we consider to be very useful or very holy. Let us obey such orders blindly, let us have *faith*, for our religious superiors are God's representatives among us, the authentic interpreters of his will.

God's will is for us to untie the beast which does not belong to us, to follow a man carrying a water jar (cf. Mk 14:13), to receive silver and gold for the Egyptians (cf. Ex 3:21-22). That is his will and our duty. Even those who command us make mistakes. His will is for us to obey them, not out of respect and submission to them, but out of respect and submission to him, since he told us to obey them. It is not difficult for him to have them change places, to have us change places, to change their hearts if he wants. We will obey him in whatever he wants from us.

Let us note however, that since we must obey them only because he wishes us to, we must also obey them to the extent that he has outlined for us. For example, he has said that we must never obey orders to do things that are *definitely* sins (when in doubt, we must still obey them because it is wise and humble for us to have more trust in their judgment than in ours), and he has ruled that in certain cases directors may be changed and we can consult a higher ecclesiastical authority, against our superior. *Faith*, absolute *faith* must guide us in everything: the superior and the director are authentic interpreters of God's will for us. We must obey them blindly as long as it does not involve definite sins, even when the order seems less than reasonable and less than perfect. We must do so by *faith*, as the apostles did here.

63. "The heavens and the earth will pass away, but my words will not pass" (Lk 21:33).

Your words, my God, are eternal truth. You have indicated with your words with what *faith* we must receive them, with what practical faith, because it is not the same to receive them with faith as to read them, even meditate on them, to tell oneself that they are beautiful and true and then to do nothing to accomplish them. If we really *believed* that Jesus' words were divine, that they were the complete truth as he said here, and elsewhere, that they are eternal and we will be judged by them, then how, unless we were mad, could we fail to devote ourselves to their practice? Yet this insanity is common among nearly all people, myself included, alas! My God, deliver me from it, make me no longer mad, but make me believe and truly enter into the spirit of the Gospel, into the practice of all your words and examples. My God, your words and examples must penetrate and inspire my whole life, Lord make it happen in me since I must have it, in you, through you and for you. Amen.

64. "Just as you enter the city, you will come upon a man carrying a water jar. Follow him into the house he enters" (Lk 22:10-11).

The apostles needed *faith* to accomplish that. It meant walking blindfolded and obeying a mysterious order. Let us obey such orders without understanding when God's will is clearly known to us. For example, if our director orders us to do something, he represents God to us, and regardless of what he tells us, we must see in his words Jesus' will. Let us bless his orders, embrace them fondly, obey him to the utmost. Perhaps if we do not understand them in the least, they will shock all our ideas, they will be the opposite of what seems perfect, wise and holy to us *(as long as they do not involve a definite sin)*. Let us obey them all the more that it is the chance to be Peter and John, to show *faith* and to comfort Jesus' heart by showing him that we *believe* in him and that we know how to obey him by obeying without understanding those who say: "He who hears you, hears me" (Lk 10:16), those whom he appoints to order us through his Spouse, the Church.

65. "This is my body, this cup is the new covenant in my blood" (Lk 22:19-20).

Oh, my God, I beg you, give me true faith in these words! If I truly *believed* them as I must fear them, what respect, what love, what passionate adoration! What deep and infinite contemplation I would have before the Holy Sacrament! Oh, how remote I would be from this half-heartedness, this indifference, this sleepiness, this dissipation, this spiritual state which does not know what to do or say, this laziness and this spiritual idleness which I so often display to you, alas, at the foot of your altar!

Help me, my God, make me see what it is, give me the eyes of faith. Oh, my Savior, if I *faithfully* looked at the tabernacle and the Holy Host, how I would drown in your love, how I would lose myself, how I would become drunk on you, to spend all the moments of my days and nights in this drunkenness which is that of truth. Oh, my God, give me this faith, a faith intense enough to make me die of love at the feet of your divine body. In you, through you and for you. Amen.

JOHN

66. "...So that everyone who believes may have eternal life in him" (Jn 3:15).

You grant salvation for *faith*, my Savior, both here and in many other places, you grant salvation for three reasons: First, *faith* is the *condition* for salvation (the condition at least "by desire"); secondly, *faith* is the *root* of salvation (it is the root, the source of love, hope and the accomplishment of the commandments and advice); third, true *faith* contains everything (faith worthy of the name contains the work dictated by faith. When we truly *believe*, we act in accordance with our belief. True faith thus contains all the love of God and people and all perfection).

My God, give me this *faith*, this deep, intense faith which makes us always act according to faith, which makes us live from faith, which bases our whole life, our thoughts, words and action on it, in other words, founding them on love and hope, truth and perfection, on you, my God! "The upright will live through faith" (Gal 3:11). My God, give me this faith!

Alas! I lacked faith when I got up late this morning. If I truly had faith that you were there, that staying awake meant being with you, have a *tete-a-tete* with you, a meeting to which you called me, not only would I have not gone back to bed, but I would have infinitely enjoyed being awake under your eyes. Forgive me, forgive me, forgive me! I lie prostrate before you, my God, and ask you for forgiveness from the depth of my soul for having been so shamefully lacking in faith and love! Forgive me, forgive me, forgive me!

Thank you for having awakened me! Thank you, help me, relieve my misery so that in the future I no longer abuse your mercy but use it to glorify you, to comfort your heart as much as I can. Do not withhold your blessings because of my unfaithfulness. Forgive me, forgive me, forgive me! Thank you!

Help me, do not withhold your blessings but increase them. Conquer evil with good, burn my ice with your heat. I am unworthy but do it for yourself: glorify your Name! And do it for me also because you love me, because no matter how bad I am, I am your child. Do it because I am asking for it on your behalf, on behalf of your Spirit, your Holy Spirit, with the humility of my contrite heart. Do not reject my prayers because you are good. "Because his mercy is eternal!" (Ps 99:5). And I ask you for the same mercy for all sinners, in you, by you and for you. Amen.

67. "No one who believes in him will be judged; but whoever does not believe is judged already" (Jn 3:18).

This concerns complete faith, which includes charity. Theoretical faith without practical faith is dead faith, according to Saint Paul. It is even an insult to God that such theoretical faith lacks practical application. It is saying to God: this is what you want from me. I know it, I believe it, but I am not doing it. Every time God grants salvation for faith, and dictates damnation for lack of faith, he refers to *complete faith*, which includes charity.

68. "Anyone who believes in the Son has eternal life, but anyone who refuses to believe in the Son will never see life: God's retribution hangs over him" (Jn 3:36).

Those who *believe*, with complete, true *faith*, not only with *thoughts* and *words*, but also with *deeds*, will have eternal life. Having faith in thought but not in words or deeds would mean not having the faith required by God, the faith glorifying God, but using the knowledge God gives us to insult him. Having faith in thoughts and words but not in deeds would be the same thing (perhaps with less impiety but with more wrong). The faith required by God is therefore necessary: faith in thoughts, words and deeds.

We must confess Jesus through this threefold expression of faith, to make it true that we have *faith*. Those who do not believe in him will not have eternal life—that is, those who do not believe in him in any way, either *implicitly or explicitly*. Those who believe in him *implicitly*, invincibly ignorant of Christianity, but believing in God as rewarding and powerful in the other life, firmly determined to do everything God asks of mankind and demonstrating this good will through their thoughts, words and deeds, believe *implicitly* in the Son of God. They believe in him *implicitly* and *confess implicitly through thoughts, words and deeds*, through an inviolable attachment to conform in thoughts, words and deeds to the will of the Father, and thus have eternal life.

But how rare is invincible ignorance of Christian revelation today! And if even the faithful experience so much difficulty believing in God and Jesus with *complete faith* in *thoughts, words* and *actions*, how many thousand times more difficult can it be for the poor unfaithful deprived of all the light, blessings and means of salvation offered by divine religion! How we must therefore pray and work (work through thoughts, words and deeds, everyone according to their own conditions and in the manner God wishes them to) to convert the unfortunate who have no knowledge of true religion! And how we must pray and work to convert all the sinners because they too lack the faith required for salvation and though somewhat less distant from God are in another sense guiltier because they abuse more of his blessings.

69. *"How can you believe, since you look to each other for glory and are not concerned with the glory that comes from the one God?" (Jn 5:44).*

Here you show, my God, how *faith* is incompatible with pride, with vain glory, with love of human esteem. In order to *believe*, we must humble ourselves, make ourselves small, admit that we have little spirit, admit a multitude of things we do not understand, obey the teachings of the Church, receive truth from it at times somewhat crudely expressed, at times from a somewhat unskilled speaker, submit our judgment, obey in spirit, and in humility be believers ourselves. Because to believe means believing we are sinners, that we can do nothing by ourselves, that every day we abuse thousands of blessings. Believing means having a divine ideal in front of us and seeing how unfortunately distant we are from it. It means seeing God's goodness and our ingratitude. *Believing* is incompatible with useless glory, human honor, seeking human esteem, because faith teaches us the opposite of all of that. It shows us the perfection of imitating a God who humbles himself to the extent of making himself human, of a God who in his hidden life was abject, persecuted, slandered and jeered at, and accused in his public life, accused, covered with disgrace in his passion and dying on the gallows of the wicked. It constantly repeats words such as: "The last shall be the first...woe to you rich...If you do not become like children, you will not enter the kingdom of heaven...any elevation is an abomination before God...I am gentle and humble of heart," and includes the parables of poor Lazarus, the Pharisee and the publican.

70. "This is carrying out God's work: you must believe in the one he has sent" (Jn 6:29).

Our Lord again makes our duty consist of faith. He does so because faith is the *beginning* of all good, it is the pure *wellspring* from where all good flows naturally. Finally, complete faith, perfect faith, such as it should be and as God requires, *is made up of the triple confession of thought, words and deeds*, in other words, all our duties. It is the beginning of all good, because only through faith may we know what our duties toward God are. It is the source of all good because it provides us with the knowledge of our duties and, through instruction, through the authority and sacraments of the Church, with the means and necessary strength to accomplish them.

Faith consists of the triple confession of thought, words and deeds (which means that it encompasses every moment of our lives and all our acts) because in order to have faith, we must first believe in thought. Otherwise, the confession of words would be a lie and deeds would have no voluntary relation to faith. We must believe in words, or we would renounce faith, which would be lying and impiety. We must conform to faith in deeds, or it would be an outrage to God, since it would appear to be saying to him: I know you and I know your teachings, but I do not care about you or them and I just act as if neither you nor they existed. Jesus therefore makes God's work consist of the complete faith of *thought, words and deeds.*

71. "It is my Father's will that whoever sees the Son and believes in him should have eternal life" (Jn 6:40).

Our Lord still grants salvation as a reward for *faith*. But by *faith* he means complete faith, which encompasses all acts in life, which not only fills the heart but extends to all words and deeds, which is such that we completely abide by "the upright will live through faith" (Gal 3:11) and that all deeds result from it. Such faith, in thought, words and deeds, is what makes all our acts be in accordance with God's will, what makes us act like saints in everything—not faith existing only deep within the soul—and for which Jesus promises eternal life. Faith without deeds is not faith; it is dead, not living, true faith.

72. "In all truth I tell you, everyone who believes has eternal life" (Jn 6:47).

Eternal life, according to our Lord, means knowing God and the one he sent, Jesus Christ (cf. Jn 17:3). Faith means eternal life in many ways. First of all, it is supreme happiness, the blessing of blessings, such great bliss that it can very well be called eternal life. In fact, what is actually the happiness of heaven? Knowing God as perfectly as our capacity to love affords in proportion to this knowledge.

And what is faith? Knowing God to a certain extent, from which a degree of love naturally ensues. Faith is what teaches us everything or nearly everything we know about God, about good and about our deeds. Faith is what gives a new outlook, new directions, what makes us live for God and not for the earth, what brings our conversation (cf. Ph 3:20) to heaven and lifts us high above the world. And if faith is true and deep, it makes us practice all virtues and consequently leads us to heaven. For who can claim to have faith if that faith is not strong enough to make one do what it commands?

Thank you my God, for this faith which you have given us and which is such a blessing, which is the source from where all other virtues in me should spring. And help me so that they do spring and so that this faith, which is such a blessing, will not be dead faith but will make me carry out your will and glorify you as much as I can at every moment of my life, in you, by you and for you. Amen! My God, please grant this great blessing of faith to all those who have not received it and make it bear fruit perfectly in those to whom you have given it. Amen.

73. *"As the Scriptures say, 'From his heart shall flow streams of living water' " (Jn 7:38).*

First of all, let us note that our Lord teaches us not only faith in himself but also in the Scriptures, since he quotes them. What is faith in our Lord? It is not simple knowledge and conviction of his existence, his divine mission, his saintliness and his divinity—a conviction similar to scientific knowledge and not guiding our deeds. This is dead faith, this is not true faith. Saint John said it clearly in his first Epistle: "To know God without practicing what he teaches means not knowing him, it means not having faith. *He who says he knows him and does not obey the commandments is a liar, and the truth is not in him. With this we are aware we know him, if we observe his teachings*" (Jn 2:4,3).

It is God himself, the Holy Spirit himself who clearly tells us through the words of Saint John, and in the Holy Scriptures and in Saint John's Gospel where faith is extensively discussed what the word *faith* means. It means complete, whole faith which stimulates not only the spirit but also the will, which transforms life, which inspires all thoughts, words and deeds, which creates the "life of the upright" and which consists not only of believing in the truth but also of accomplishing all good, of the holiness of life, of as true an existence as allowed by human frailty and of the divine teachings in which we believe.

The *faith* to which Jesus and Saint John refer here means not only believing but living in accordance with one's beliefs. And those who thus believe not only in spirit but in all acts of their lives will spread good around them and will be a source of blessings for their neighbors. They will not go alone to God but will be followed by a procession of souls. Their lips, hearts and words will be living waters spreading eternal life, spreading good in souls, creating conversions and sanctification. Their speeches will be streams of living water flowing to eternal life (cf. Jn 7:38).

Those who believe without practicing, who believe in truth but not saintliness, can speak and speak well, can tell the truth and tell it well, but their words will bear no fruit. The water is beautiful but sterile and produces no virtue, nothing which ascends to heaven. The words of those who believe and act, who believe and are saintly, may seem poor and contemptible on the surface. They may seem like a thin trickle of water or a river but actually their fruits are always abundant. They give life and everything they water blossoms upwards and grows high and full of life and beauty toward heaven. If we wish to do good to souls, let us be saints. My God, give me this faith.

74. *"I am the light of the world; anyone who follows me will not be walking in the dark but will have the light of life" (Jn 8:12).*

Oh my God, if we had *faith* in these words, as we should have faith in the Word of God, how our thoughts and lives would be different! How we would imitate your examples! How we would practice your teachings! How our lives would reflect yours! How we would *follow* you in darkness, poverty, abjection, manual work and silence,

Learning silence from you,
To pass unnoticed on earth
Like a traveler at night.

How all of us who have not *received a mission* from your Church to preach the Gospel and lead your public life would throw ourselves into absolute imitation of your life in Nazareth, shrouding ourselves, disappearing with you into this infinite darkness, into this apparent uselessness, silently offering our prayers to God for the salvation of all people, useless in the eyes of the world but "earthworms and abjection of the people" (Ps 21:7). This was your life for thirty years, and you did not find it to be beneath you; would it be beneath us? Oh, no! On the contrary, it would be above us, with its hidden greatness, but unworthy as we are let us still imitate this divine life since you invite us to do so, with *faith* in its beauty, with *faith* in its greatness, with *faith* that by following it, by following you, we are not walking in darkness but have the light of life. My God, give me *this faith*!

75. *"Even if you refuse to believe in me, at least believe in the work I do; then you will know for certain that the Father is in me and I am in the Father" (Jn 10:38).*

...Since faith is, so to speak, indispensable for salvation, and since our Lord takes such pains to inspire it in people, let us do our utmost to help those who don't have it obtain it. All of us can work at this task, if only through prayer, penitence and living holy lives. And we should all work at it with all the means, according to our condition, that God wishes us to use. Let us therefore ardently wish for all people to have faith. Let us try with all our God-granted powers to make those lacking it obtain it and to develop it in those who already have it. Because there can never be enough of the faith through which "the upright live" (Gal 3:11).

At the same time let us thank God for having given it to us, let us pray for him to develop it in us, and let us ask forgiveness for having been so often unfaithful in practice, in thinking, speaking and acting according to human appearances and judgments, instead of thinking, speaking and acting according to faith. And let us take care in the future to live by faith ourselves and to try to make others do so. I place these wishes at your feet, at the feet of the nativity,

Lord Jesus. Bless them and make me faithful to these resolutions that I am making for your sake. Lord Jesus, make me and your children live by faith in this world, and thereby comfort your sacred Heart as much as we can, in you, by you and for you. Amen! Holy Virgin, Saint Joseph, present this prayer to the One who wants to be your Child and place us at his feet, in the midst of all of you.

76. "Anyone who believes in me, even though that person dies, will live, and whoever lives and believes in me will never die" (Jn 11:25-26).

Those who believe in you, divine Infant Jesus, whom I adore in the nativity, during this sweet Christmas season, those who believe in you with *complete faith*, with faith accompanied by *good deeds*, with a faith which *inspires my whole life*, with a faith through which the upright live (because this is the meaning of the word *faith* here and generally in Saint John, see first epistle of Saint John), even if they are dead in the eyes of people, in reality they live because the separation of soul and body is not death for them but the continuation of life, the continuation of the life of divine love in which "the upright live through faith" which they led here on earth, or better yet the heightening of their lives, since "eternal life is to know you, the only true God and Jesus Christ whom you have sent" (Jn 17:3).

The upright already lived here on earth, since they "lived through this faith" and this knowledge, but their lives became infinitely more abundant when their souls left their bodies, since at that moment they saw God and Jesus clearly and "face to face" and knew them perfectly, according to the capacity of their nature, while here on earth they only caught a brief glimpse of them "like in a mirror." They therefore live, they are not dead.

Those who live and believe, who believe with a faith accompanied by charity and good deeds, who live and "live through faith," shall never die, since their lives, which consist of knowing God and Jesus, far from being extinguished or diminishing, will become a thousand times more intense at the moment the soul and body separate. Far from being death, this moment will be a marvelous heightening of life, an entry into light after the first light of dawn, the radiant sunrise after the shadows of moonlight and dusk. This will be the passage from a winter day to a day "as bright as seven days," to a "sun as brilliant as seven suns" (Is 30:26).

My God, how good you are! And how sweet your promises are! Oh good Jesus, what goodness you have brought us! And how little you ask in return! And alas! How poorly I give. Help me, sweet Infant Jesus, so that in the future I return the goodness to you with all the perfection within me and give the same blessing to all your children, in you, by you and for you. Holy Virgin, Saint Joseph, Holy Angels, pray for us that we may do so.

77. "I say this for the people who hear me, so they will believe you have sent me" (Jn 11:42).

My Lord, you make this great miracle only or mainly because we *believe* in your divine mission. How good you are, to have done and said so many wonders to give us this infinite blessing of faith! And how good you are to add more wonders everyday by continuously speaking to our hearts to make us believe more strongly! How good you are to create so many divine miracles in souls to stimulate and nurture faith! All this, my God, must penetrate us through the infinite value of faith, through the gratefulness we owe you for the faults we have committed against it, through the desire to increasingly live by faith in the future and to work with all our powers and all the means God grants us to help others obtain the infinite blessing of faith.

78. "Unless a wheat grain falls into the earth and dies, it remains only a single grain; but if it dies it yields a rich harvest" (Jn 12:24-25).

Oh my God, if we truly had *faith* in these words, how we would embrace *suffering*, penitence, through which you provide all means of helping souls! You must be referring to *suffering* here, my divine Jesus, since you are discussing your Passion here. My sweet Jesus, you who call us so forcefully with these words to *suffering*, give me *faith*, making me always have them before my eyes, making my life conform despite the revulsion and revolt of nature, despite the demon's specious reasoning and illusions. Give me *faith* making me die through penitence and suffering and, if it is your holy will, as a martyr, thus making my life resemble yours and giving it a *similarity with yours*, which you made my special calling.

You suffered so much in your soul from the sins and pain of your children and in your body from cold, fatigue, hunger and thirst, from lack of sleep and everything that comes with a life of penitence, from poverty, hard work, abjection and evangelical journeys which you embraced from the cradle to the cross. My divine Jesus, make me suffer with *faith* in your words, *faith* in your examples, to obey you, resemble you, to make as many worthy sacrifices within my power, as you have done; to do the best possible good I can, as you have done. Give me *faith* in these solemn words, and give me *the tasks which must follow this faith*. I ask you on my knees at the foot of the nativity, through the Holy Virgin, Saint Joseph, Saint Magdalene, Saint Paul, my guardian Angel, sweet Infant Jesus, divine and beloved Infant Jesus! Amen!

79. *"I have come into the world as light, to prevent anyone who believes in me from staying in the dark anymore" (Jn 12:46).*

Thank you, my God, for so clearly explaining to us the effect of faith! Yes, it is a light. In its brightness we can distinguish a thousand new objects of which we had previously been completely unaware. In its brightness, the objects which we had already glimpsed in the darkness and fog of our poor human reason alone appear as they truly are, in their true greatness, their true shapes, their true colors. Without faith we are in darkness, we walk in the night, bumping into thousands of obstacles, dimly glimpsing as fantastic images whatever touches us and not seeing what is the slightest bit away from us.

Faith illuminates these shadows like a bright sun. It makes our path appear, everything is visible, whatever is near is flooded with light, and whatever is far, although not seen as distinctly, is clearly visible. The destination on our path can be seen from afar, not as a vacillating light burning far away in the night, but as a great city, far from us but well in sight, with its dazzling walls crowning a high mountain. We can see it from all directions and it shines in all directions; from all directions we can see the thousand avenues leading to it. It is the great sun and the great light.

How good you are, my God, to have so completely dispelled the deep darkness and replaced it with such bright light—first by coming to earth and then by giving me the blessed light of faith! Thank you, thank you, thank you! My Lord, give it to all people and preserve it in them. I ask you on my knees at the feet of the nativity, in you, by you and for you, through the Holy Virgin and Saint Joseph. Oh sweet Jesus, divine Infant Jesus, oh beloved and sweet Infant Jesus.

80. "What scripture says must be fulfilled: He who shares my table takes advantage of me" (Jn 13:18).

What faith we must have in the Scriptures, in every single word. We learn it through the Church and Jesus teaches it to us with his words: "I have come not to abolish [the Law or the Prophets] but to complete them" (Mt 5:17). "Not one dot, not one little stroke is to disappear from the Law until its purpose is achieved. Heaven and earth will pass away but my word will not pass" (Mt 5:18). But he proves this truth to us through practice itself, with extreme power. Let us therefore believe everything that has been written in the Scriptures. Let us truly have *faith* in it. And let it teach us the truth to that point. *Let us read it, contemplate it and try to understand it* as best as possible in order to know and to love God as much as possible through it and in order to understand our duty as best as possible through it. And since its teachings are the truth itself, *let us practice them.*

Give me this *faith*, oh sweet Jesus, give it to all your children. I ask you at the feet of the nativity, at this hour when all sleep except Mary and Joseph who lovingly watch over you at your feet, lost in your adoration and your love, lost and drowned in your blessed contemplation. I ask you through their intercession, in you, by you and for you, oh beloved Jesus, oh sweet Infant Jesus!

81. "I tell you this now, before it happens, so that when it does happen, you may believe that I am He" (Jn 13:19).

A few lines above you resurrected Lazarus to confirm your divine mission, your divinity, through miracles. Now you confirm it with a prophecy: You make miracles and predictions to give us *faith*. Oh! What a price you set for faith through such prodigies, for which you promise salvation, and hell to those who refuse it, since establishing faith in souls is such a large part of your work and that of the Church's here on earth.

Let us have faith, a practicing faith, faith "through which the upright live" (Gal 3:11) inspiring all thoughts, words and deeds. Let us be grateful for what God has given us and do everything within our power to develop it in ourselves, to develop it or create it in others. Let us do what God wants us to do to inspire the unfortunate who lack faith. This is one of our purposes on earth.

82. "Do not let your hearts be troubled. You trust in God, trust also in me" (Jn 14:1).

Peace, serenity, trust and contentment in everything, perpetual blessing and divine aid are indeed some of the first effects, the necessary effects, of *faith*. What does faith teach us? "Everything that happens, happens with God's permission or by his will. God sees everything that happens and he either makes it happen or lets it happen. God loves us, he loves all people and allows this or that to happen. Everything that happens, happens for the benefit of the chosen. Not a hair shall fall from our heads without God's will.

Let us seek God and his righteousness and all the rest will be given us besides. Let us not concern ourselves with eating, drinking or clothing. Let us seek the kingdom of God and our heavenly Father will give us all the rest. Let us not worry about tomorrow, for every day is enough in itself. Happy are the poor who are hungry, those who cry and those persecuted by justice. Do not marry. May those reveling in joy act as if they are not and those who cry as if they are not crying. The face of this world will pass. Our comfort rests in heaven. We are enshrouded with Jesus in God." Those who believe in God and in Jesus believe this and many other comforting truths. How could trouble enter a soul founded on such *faith*?

83. "Whoever believes in me will perform the same works as I do myself and will perform even greater works, because I am going to the Father. Whatever you ask for in my name I will do, so that the Father may be glorified in the Son" (Jn 14:12-13).

My Lord, here you promised the gift of miracle-making to those who believe in you. Does this mean that all people who truly have faith, faith worthy of the name, together with love and charity, will receive the gift of miracle-making?

This passage can be understood in two ways. It certainly promises the gift of miracle-making to apostles, provided they have faith, because these words were addressed to them. Jesus said them after the Last Supper when the apostles were alone with him. What he said directly and definitely concerns them. He ordered them to believe in him and in return for their faith he promised them the gift of miracle-making. As for the faithful in general, he also appears to have promised them but on the condition that they have sufficient, true faith, along with deeds, charity and virtues which necessarily stem from *true* faith and above all *humility*. Humility appears to be the first, natural and necessary effect of true faith. How can we believe in God, in everything he is and believe that we are something? If faith is great enough, if the virtues which make up *this true faith* are deep enough for it to be *faith*, God will grant the requested miracle. This is what appears to come out of these words and commentary provided by the example of the saints.

84. "I have told you this now, before it happens, so that when it does happen you may believe" (Jn 14:29).

Our Lord repeats that the reason for all his prophecies and miracles is mainly to establish a sound foundation for the faith of his disciples. How he acts, what great deeds he achieves, what advice he repeats, how he lavishes his words and deeds, are all divine deeds, prophecies and miracles which serve to give his disciples solid faith! These deeds and words are also directed at us. Let us benefit from them and also have unshakable faith inspiring all our acts at every moment of our lives. Since Jesus did so much to inspire faith in people, if we wish to imitate him we too must do all we can, everything our leaders advise us to and tell us is God's will working to convert people, to develop or create *faith* in them. Give me this divine aid, oh divine Infant Jesus, at the feet of the crib where I write these words, and develop faith in me, instill it in my soul as you want it to be and make me work toward doing so for others, as you wish of me, my Master, my beloved Lord, my dear Sovereign, you for whom alone I want to breathe every moment of my life, to whose service and will I want to devote every moment of my life, for whom I would unhesitatingly live or die, oh divine Jesus, oh sweet Infant Jesus! I ask you for this twofold blessing through the intercession of my sweet parents, Mary and Joseph, of my two parents, Saint Magdalene and Saint Paul, of my guardian Angel. Grant it to me from the nativity, in you, by you and for you, oh dearest one, oh sweet divine Infant Jesus!

85. "Because the Father himself loves you for loving me and believing that I came from God" (Jn 16:27).

Here you give *faith* accompanied by charity the power to earn the Father's love. It is not enough to think we love the Son as a human being, that we admire him. We must admire him enough to see him as more than a man and love him not as we would love a human being but with the love we owe God.

When *we believe* in your Son as we should *believe* in him and *love* him as we should love him, then we are truly his friend, his faithful servant, his devoted disciple. And by the natural effect of the Father's love for the Son, the Father loves the friends, the faithful servants, the devoted disciples and the true friends of his Son. But the Father loves the Son too much to be able to love those who, although aware of what they owe the Son, do not fulfill the tasks they owe him. This is one of the causes of "outside of faith, outside of the Church, no salvation is possible."[8] It is because the Father loves the Son too much to love and receive as his own those who—aware of who the Son is and called to him through the grace of his Father and his messengers—have too much ill will, indifference or cowardice to recognize the Son for what he is and grant him the tasks and love they owe him. The Father loves the Son too much to be able to love such people.

86. "So that the world may believe it was you who sent me" (Jn 17:21).

On the banks of the Cedron Jesus prayed to his Father for all people to have *faith* in his supreme prayer. He did so much to inspire this faith, these countless miracles, prophecies and predictions. When he left this world, he made a final effort to give faith to all people, delegating part of this task to his Father and the part to his disciples, placing in their hands, so to speak, the supreme tool to obtain it: prayer. Let us therefore work like Jesus worked and for him to give faith to people. Let us use all the means he wishes of us and, above all, prayer, which is the means for every person everyday.

---

[8]*Cf. S. Cyprien, Ep. 73,* ad Jubaianum, 21.

87. "They then led Jesus from the house of Caiaphas to the Praetorium" (Jn 18:28).

My Lord Jesus, if we truly had *faith* in these words, how fearless we would be of contempt, insults and humiliation. How we would love them and seek them out in order to be similar to you! How we would flee human esteem, consideration, honor, everything that seems great in people's eyes! How we would love abjection, and cherish all humiliation, if we truly had *faith* in Jesus' infinite humiliations!

88. "Pilate then had Jesus taken away and scourged" (Jn 19:1).

Oh my God, if we truly had *faith* in these words, if we *believed* in what you suffered for us, how we would throw ourselves into mortification, how we would desire, love and seek suffering, in order to resemble you! How your disciples would be other than what they are! How we would fast and how austere our meals would be! How we would rejoice in sickness instead of seeking first to avoid or to cure it! How all physical or spiritual suffering would be blessed, cherished, savored and welcomed by us! My Lord Jesus, who from the cradle to the cross have not ceased during your life to preach mortification, suffering and the cross to me and to cry out to me so loudly of your Passion, give me *faith* in your suffering, make me *believe* in it, listen to its voice and let me also suffer like you, with my wish to imitate you as much and however you want me to, in you, by you and for you, my adored Lord Jesus!

89. "And bowing his head he gave up his spirit" (Jn 19:30).

My Lord Jesus, you died and died for us! If we truly had *faith* in that, how we would want to die and to die as martyrs. How we would want to die suffering instead of fearing death, to die as if nothing on earth could frighten us because the worst thing anyone could do to us would be to make us die suffering terrible pain. But such a death, received in accordance with your will and love, would be a perfect blessing, an imitation thrice blessed by you, my divine Jesus.

For whatever reason they killed us, if in spirit we received unjust and cruel death, like a blessed gift by your hand, if we thanked you for it like a sweet blessing, as a blessed imitation of your end, if we offered it to you like a sacrifice offered in good will, if we did not resist in order to obey your words "offer no resistance to the wicked" (Mt 5:39), and following your example "like a lamb led to the slaughter-house, like a sheep before its shearers, he never opened his mouth" (Is 53:7), then whatever reason they had to kill us, we would die in pure love and our death would be a sweet sacrifice to you. While we would not be martyrs in the strict sense of the word, and in the eyes of others, we would be martyrs in your eyes and that would be a perfect reflection of your death and a very loving end which would take us straight to heaven.

For if we didn't in this case offer our blood for our faith, we would have offered it with all our hearts and delivered it for your love. Oh divine Infant Jesus, at whose feet I kneel before your little crib, should it be your will, give me the infinite blessing of a martyr's death soon. And while waiting, make me ardently desire it in you, for you and by you. But above all, let me comfort you as much as possible during every moment of my life and by my death. And I ask the same blessing for all your children, oh blessed and beloved sweet Infant Jesus. How I love and adore you with all my heart! Amen!

90. "You believe because you can see me. Blessed are those who have not seen and yet believe" (Jn 20:29).

Thomas only believed upon seeing *proof*. We should not require *proof* in order to believe. We *must* believe in Jesus, in everything that religion teaches us as soon as we are *certain* of the truth of Christianity. The more serious a task, the more it requires we accomplish it with haste as soon as we are sufficiently aware of it.

Requiring more than reasonable awareness on the part of a superior to accomplish this order, asking for proof before accomplishing it so we have enough moral certainty and evidence to assure ourselves of it, is insolence toward this superior, a deliberate harmful delay in carrying out his commandment and ill will and disdain of his orders. Thus when we are certain that God has made a revelation and ordered us to believe it, requiring *proof* of this order is ill will, a deliberate delay in carrying it out and disdain of his orders.

The more we owe obedience to someone, the more we must obey that person upon the slightest sign or word. The more we love someone, the more ready we are to accomplish whatever that person wants with a word. To require *proof* of the order is on the contrary proof of very little obedience and very little love. Before God, supreme obedience and supreme love, we would be very guilty of not wanting to believe what he orders us to believe except if we had *proof* of his order. We must make certain not to make mistakes, not to do anything other than what he wants of us, to believe in a voice other than his. But as soon as we are *certain* that he commands us to believe, let us believe with all our soul in this commandment and whatever he wants us to believe.

...other New City Press publications

The Silent Witness
by Sergius Lorit

3rd printing

"Some have called him the unknown disciple of Christ; others, the greatest saint of our times, a mystic explorer, an adventurer, a disarmed prophet, a father and contemplative of the desert, and, finally, a martyr. For the writer, Foucauld (1858-1916) was all these and more—a fun loving youth, an officer in the French army, a Trappist monk for 15 years, and finally a contemplative in the Sahara....

This book describes Foucauld, the 'universal brother,' for those who wish to know more about his life and spirituality." *Messenger of St. Anthony*
0-911-882-29-X, 174 pp

Meditations
by Chiara Lubich

6th printing

"Millions throughout the world have been inspired by the gospel meditations of Chiara Lubich, foundress of the Focolare Movement. *Meditations* is another collection of brief but intensely meaningful thoughts carefully mined from the Scriptures. Like shafts of sunlight that brake through the clouds on a dreary day, these meditations touch us and turn our most mundane activities into brightly lit God-moments...." *Liguorian*
0-911782-20-6, 134 pp

My Life with Jesus
by André Sève

"Christianity can be summed up in one name: Jesus Christ. More than a set of teachings, the Gospel is a person: the Word made flesh. In this book, the author leads the reader directly toward He who for the Christian is the source and completion of all things; the Alpha and the Omega." *(an excerpt from the book)*
0-911782-52-4, 207 pp

Thirty Minutes for God
by André Sève

"Arguments about whether we should or should not meditate daily are rather futile because they sidetrack us from the true question. It's not a matter of adding something more to my day or of being initiated into a spiritual technique. It's a matter of the all-encompassing meaning I want to give my life. Either hunger for God is the sun around which I organize everything; or else God is just one object among others orbiting the very crowded sky of my life." *(an excerpt from the book)*
0-911782-49-4, 125 pp

Reaching for More
by Pascal Foresi

"This is a book of keen spiritual insights and solid guidance for all committed Christians. Father Foresi...bases himself on the Bible, the Fathers of the Church, and the teachings of the Second Vatican Council, to delineate what it means to be a Christian in today's world. His many years of ministry to lay people, priests, and religious, have encouraged him to write a book that is full of hope for the future." *Messenger of St. Anthony*
0-911782-40-0, 158 pp

Diary of Fire
by Igino Giordani

"The author began his life as a bricklayer, worked as a journalist against Fascism, and spent the last 30 years of his life consecrated to the Focolare Movement, the first married person to do so. His diary begins during World War II as if in a furnace and is incandescent with yearning for God and with wonderfully sensible convictions about holiness in the world. Giordani has recorded the kind of truth that the fire of prayer refines. His prayer seems to have been what Ignatius Loyola would call 'consideration,' and everyone of his pages is alive, though he died at 85 in 1980." *America*
0-911782-41-9, 118 pp

Diary 1964/65
by Chiara Lubich

In addition to the story of events and encounters at the time of Vatican II, this is a journey of the soul. These are the innermost thoughts and reflections of a wayfarer constantly listening to the Holy Spirit, constantly sharing the spirituality of unity based on Jesus in the midst.
0-911782-55-9, 176 pp